UNDEFEATED: Fro

"If life has dealt you a hard blow and you're wondering where God is in the midst of your trials, this book will help you get on the trail to triumph."

Kary Oberbrunner, author of *Elixir Project, Day Job to Dream Job, The Deeper Path* and *Your Secret Name*

"When we speak of victory, we must remember that victory comes only after a battle is fought. We must endure the chaos as we wage war with the trials thrown our way. God's plan is for our good yet we must choose to get up and walk through the battleground to reach our victory. For victory is ours! Jesus won the ultimate battle on the cross for each one of us. So walk confidently through that battlefield you see before you.

Elizabeth Meyers speaks from her personal experience of walking the battlefield following the loss of a child. Unbearable pain. Black voids open and pull you in as your earth falters under your very feet and you feel defeated, dejected, desperate and depressed.

If you are walking the path of loss now, read *UNDEFEATED: From Trial to Triumph, How to Stop Fighting the Wrong Battles and Start Living Victoriously*. Jesus Christ is the one walking hand in hand with you as you walk towards your victory because, 'Victory is Mine' says the Lord.

Choose to triumph over your trials. Having a strategy as you enter the battleground is powerful. That is what *UNDEFEATED* gives you - battle strategy and tactics.

Live Victoriously!"

Susan B. Mead, award winning author of *Dance with Jesus: From Grief to Grace*
A mom who buried her "forever 20" year old son, Kyle, yet lives victoriously today
SusanBMead.com

"Within these pages you will find raw transparency and incredible inspiration. Elizabeth has taken the time to so bravely and honestly share her life and heart here and I can promise you that you will be greatly blessed and encouraged by her words."

Tai East, creator and writer of *A SPIRIT-Kissed Soul*
aspiritkissedsoul.wordpress.com

The STAND STRONG Book Series

Book One
UNDEFEATED: From Trial to Triumph
How to Stop Fighting the Wrong Battles and Start Living Victoriously

Book Two
UNDAUNTED: Your Battle Plan for Victorious Living
Winning in Life by Building a Strong Spirit, Soul, and Body

Book Three
UNSHAKABLE: Stand Strong Even When Your World Gets Rocked
Building a Biblical Foundation for an Unshakable Faith in an Unbeatable God

Watch for the next two books in the STAND STRONG series.
Available soon wherever books are sold!
Visit StandStrongFaith.com to get the most up-to-date information.

STAND STRONG SERIES
BOOK ONE

UNDEFEATED

From Trial to Triumph

How to Stop Fighting the Wrong Battles and
Start Living Victoriously

Susan
STAND STRONG
I cor 15:57-58
elizabeth myus

ELIZABETH MEYERS

**⌐AUTHOR ⌐elite
ACADEMY**

Printed in the United States of America

Published by Author Academy Elite
P.O. Box 43, Powell, OH 43035

www.AuthorAcademyElite.com

Paperback ISBN-13: 978-1-64085-087-3
Hardback ISBN-13: 978-1-64085-085-9
Library of Congress Control Number: 2017911801

Cover design by: Jelena Jovanovic (LadyElizia)
Author photo by: Larissa Photography

Dedicated to my precious son,

Timothy

whose brief life brought me the gift of brokenness
and the courage to strive toward wholeness
so that I might find meaning in his life and my pain.

Stand Strong Faith Online

Visit the website!

Please visit StandStrongFaith.com for supplementary resources to support you as you stand strong in your faith. There you will find free printables, prayers, scriptures, playlists, and other tools to help you fortify your faith to live UNDEFEATED, UNDAUNTED, and UNSHAKABLE.

Please email elizabeth@standstrongfaith.com with your questions, comments, feedback or suggestions.

Share the love!

Do you want your friends and loved ones to live undefeated too? If you enjoyed this book, please consider telling others about it, sharing it on social media, or giving a copy to a friend in need. Thank you!

Join the conversation!

Use *#standstrongfaith* & *#undefeatedbook* on social media to share what you've learned and how you are living undefeated!

CONTENTS

UNDEFEATED: From Trial to Triumph

How to Stop Fighting the Wrong Battles and Start Living Victoriously

PART I

UNDONE:
THE WAY OF TRIALS

Life can be chaotic and confusing.
Choosing to believe in spite of uncertainty gives you a firm place
to stand strong with unshakable faith.

Then said I, Woe is me! for I am undone.
~ Isaiah 6:5, KJV

Many people find themselves shaken because of circumstances beyond their control. Sometimes, faith and reality collide and slam hard into one another, leaving us breathless and bruised. Our faith can falter when our mind is full of unanswerable questions and nagging doubts.

Though it is uncomfortable, undone is the best place to be, for when we are undone, we no longer depend on ourselves but on God alone. It is when we are weak that He shows Himself strong through us, accomplishing for us what we know we could never do for ourselves. So don't freak out when you become undone. You are not weak or faithless. You are human. Embrace your uncertainty and let your need draw you closer to God.

CHAPTER 1

CONFLICTED: WHEN FAITH AND REALITY COLLIDE

Navigating Uncharted Waters

*"Suffering is no sign that God has abandoned us;
adversity is no evidence of condemnation."*
~ Eugene Peterson

Collision

I held my son's lifeless body in the palm of my hand, sobbing with the raw intensity of fresh grief. He had been born into the arms of Jesus, bypassing my arms altogether.

I was four months pregnant with our sixth child and had finally looked past my exhaustion and fear to believe this child within me was a blessing and not a burden.

My head knew that already, but my emotions had been stubbornly refusing to follow. I was overwhelmed with multiple simultaneous life stressors and thought I deserved a break from pregnancy and nursing long enough to get through our next military move.

Now my son was gone too soon, and I had not fully appreciated his presence while he was with me.

I remember sobbing on my husband's shoulder while holding our baby's body. I have never heard myself cry like that before or since. It did not even sound human to me. It did not sound like me at all.

We named our son Timothy.

That was the day I crossed the threshold into the darkest season of my life. My emptiness and sorrow plunged me into a dark abyss of despair and fear cloaked by a busy life and a practiced smile.

Fair-Weather Faith

For many years before that traumatic day, I had what I considered to be a strong faith in God and the truth of His Word. Everything in life seemed to line up exactly with what I read in my Bible. I had no reason to doubt that all His promises were true.

Just a couple of months before my son's death, I had felt connected with God so much closer than ever before. When I prayed, I truly felt that we were meeting in an intimate conversation. I felt like I was on a mountaintop with God. I had an incredible view and a sense of significance. I sensed God at work all around me and was thrilled at the prospect of being used by Him to minister to the people around me.

I thought my foundation in Christ was solid. I had built my life upon the Rock, and I remained convinced that no storm would be able to shake me. But that was before the bottom dropped out of my life and I went careening over the edge of my faith, free falling in confusion, and hitting the rocks at the bottom of a dark valley in unbearable pain.

Faith, Meet Reality

We had no rest, but we were harassed at every turn—
conflicts on the outside, fears within.
~ 2 Corinthians 7:5, NIV

The month before my son's passing, I entered a year-long battle where I felt attacked and defeated at every turn. Nothing seemed to work out the way it should. I endured a series of personal tragedies of all shapes and sizes which left me completely undone. The abrupt end of my pregnancy negatively impacted my health, and I was left anemic and exhausted.

I needed to rest to heal physically, but I also needed to re-engage with my other children and my life so I could heal emotionally. It was a catch-22. I had to sacrifice one to heal the other, and I could never quite find a balance. I got stuck, unable to move forward in any meaningful way.

Suddenly, miserable reality and the shining faith I had held for so long would simply not cooperate with one another. They collided with each other in brutal ways that shredded my heart, twisted my thinking, and weakened my will.

I imagine it was not unlike how Job must have felt experiencing repeated bad news and trials in wave after unrelenting wave. The devil loves to kick us when we're down, and he was having a heyday with me. As if losing my son wasn't heartbreak enough, that was only the beginning. The hits just kept coming—infections, pests, more death, strife, struggle, and complete mental, emotional, and physical exhaustion.

Collateral Damage

Our enemy also loves to isolate us. It's easier for him to pick us off one at a time that way. I felt more alone during my season of intense grief than I ever had before or since. My unique social situation and nature of my loss left me without much emotional support.

As a military family, we move frequently. During this desperate time of my life, we were in a transition period, so a network of supportive friends was virtually non-existent. We were far away from family, and we were just meeting a slew of new people who didn't even know that I had been pregnant, much less that it had ended suddenly and tragically.

I quickly discovered that when you are meeting new people for the first time, it's best to pretend all is well. Although my pain was still very raw, I learned to hide it. When I didn't, and the truth of my broken heart slipped out, people would awkwardly whisper, "oh," and move away from me in uncomfortable silence.

It turns out nobody is comfortable talking about dead babies. Even though estimates claim that 25% of women suffer pregnancy loss, we are somehow expected never to mention it. It makes people feel uneasy. People prefer to live in a pretend world where unborn babies don't die unexpectedly.

When asked about my children, I always had the internal struggle of whether to mention Timmy or not. Speaking of him created an awkward silence that isolated me even more. Not speaking of him felt like I was disowning my son, sealing shut the relief valve on the agony building pressure within me. Avoiding people altogether became much less hurtful than seeking any companionship or understanding from them.

Furthermore, because my son was not yet 20 weeks old when he died, he was not even considered human from a medical standpoint. There was no official or legal acknowledgment of his death, and no opportunity for a funeral. The hospital staff refused to turn his body back over to me.

Everyone I interacted with at the hospital insisted on referring to him as P.O.C., or "products of conception." Never mind the fact that I was holding a tiny body undeniably human in every way. Everyone apparently refused to acknowledge there had been a death, because to do so would mean there had been a human life involved. It seemed to me that to acknowledge another woman's right to choose, they completely denied my right to grieve.

No matter where I turned, I could not find anyone who was willing or able to mourn with me or even let me mourn in their presence. Others' incapacity to validate my grief and acknowledge my suffering spread the cracks in my broken heart ever wider.

I incorrectly assumed that God had abandoned me too. If He cared about me, then He would have sent people to care for me, I reasoned. Apparently, God was indifferent to my pain. He was hauntingly silent when I cried out in despair. Broken and angry, I pulled away from Him too.

Faith Untethered

My faith had hit reality like a brick wall. Caught off guard, I was left stunned, hurt, and confused. I descended into a dark pit at the bottom of a deep valley. It was the Valley of the Shadow of Death—the death of my baby, my health, my hope, my energy, and eventually, even the death of my faith in the God that was supposed to be all-powerful and full of love. Where was God?

I couldn't find a firm foothold for my faith. Why did God seem so distant when I needed Him most? What good was the promise of His presence if I was unable to sense it? Why did He keep refusing to shield me from all the debris and broken glass that was flying against me? And when would this awful storm **ever** end?

My Fair-Weather Faith had become a Faith Untethered, flapping violently in the wind like a tattered flag torn by the storm. When faith and reality collided, I got crunched in-between. I was broken, bruised, and bloodied by brutal realities of life that I was unable to reconcile with the God I thought I knew. Even after the storm outside calmed and subsided, the storm within me raged on.

> My Fair-Weather Faith had become a Faith Untethered, flapping violently in the wind like a tattered flag torn by the storm.

Reading my Bible seemed to unravel my faith rather than bolster it. I would read passages like:

If you say, "The Lord is my refuge," and you make the Most High your dwelling, no harm will overtake you, no disaster will come near your tent. For he will command his angels concerning you to guard you in all your ways; they will lift you up in their hands, so that you will not strike your foot against a stone. You will tread on the lion and the cobra; you will trample the great lion and the serpent.
~ Psalm 91: 9-13, NIV

Secretly, I thought, "That's not true; at least not for me, anyway." I'm the one getting trampled.

I remember having the awful and arrogant thought, "Well, Lord, if this is how You treat Your friends, I'm not so sure I want to be counted among them anymore." I still went through all the motions of being a dedicated Christian, but on the inside, I felt as lost as a saved person could be. To me, the promise of an abundant life had left me nothing but a hollow shell.

I struggled to keep my faith afloat and failed more often than I succeeded. God seemed distant and silent. His promises felt hollow and full of false hopes.

Collision Avoidance

In the years that followed, I continued to tread water, desperately trying to stay afloat—not making any visible headway but just trying not to sink completely. Even after the attacks subsided, the effects lingered on for years. I still bear the scars.

Even people who knew me well had no idea how bad I was hurting because I didn't let them. I had learned to hide my sorrow for the sake of others early on, and somehow it was a very hard habit to break.

I forced myself to power gracefully through life like a ballerina on stage who smiles through the pain, the strain and the stretching of her performance. But it was just that—a performance. In the backstage recesses of my life, behind the pretty curtains presented to public view, I was slowly suffocating under the strain of a despair that would not budge no matter how hard I tried to move it or pray my way out from under it.

The pressure of my mental, emotional, and spiritual burdens literally weighed me down so that I was always physically fatigued. Despite my utter exhaustion during the day, I was unable to sleep at night, kept awake by huge unanswerable questions and a gnawing indefinite anxiety.

My life was a battleground, and I felt attacked, harassed, and thoroughly defeated on every front. I was stuck. The longer I lived in the land of Self-Pity, the more I swallowed the enemy's lies, and the harder it was to keep faking it. Something had to give.

Courage to Change

Why am I so depressed? Why this turmoil within me? Put your hope in God, for I will still praise Him, my Savior and my God.
~ Psalm 43:5, HCSB

We are only motivated to change our ways when the pain of staying as we are exceeds the pain of making necessary but difficult changes in our lives. After five years, two moves, and three more babies, my burden was finally too crushing to carry alone in silence anymore. The time to change course had come.

I pushed through the embarrassment of admitting, "I'm not okay"—to family, to friends, to my pastor, and to professionals. I laid down my pride of wanting to be perfect and self-sufficient. I decided to be more proactive about seeking help instead of waiting for God to drop deliverance in my lap while pouting and giving Him the cold shoulder when He didn't.

I sought pastoral care and professional help. I made self-care a higher priority, no small feat for a mother of eight! I finally admitted that I have to take care of myself to take care of my family. But most importantly, I humbly turned my heart and my mind to God again, realizing there was nowhere else to go to find answers but back to the One who made me (John 6:68).

A Firm New Foundation

As I cried out to God for relief, for answers, and for rescue, there was no dramatic turning point—nothing movie-worthy. But bit by bit, God tore down my rickety, unstable foundation that I had built on everything going my way.

> For where there are shadows, there is always a Light somewhere.

Slowly, He began to rebuild a much stronger foundation built on His unshakable truths, unwavering faithfulness, and undying love.

I know now that I was never abandoned as I thought or as alone as I felt for I never walked alone.

Even when I was sure He had forsaken me, He was still leading me through the shadowy places of Death's Valley of Tears. For where there are shadows, there is always a Light somewhere.

He always goes before me to guide me and smooth the way, behind me to guard against what I cannot perceive, and beside me to sustain my weary feet along the way. In every trial and storm and anguish, He has already been there and now guides me through, picking me up when I fall.

It has been ten years since my son's sudden death. Ten years is a long time. The adage is not true. Time does not heal all wounds. Untreated wounds fester and spread their poison to other areas. Jesus heals all wounds but always in His perfect timing, and only when we finally allow Him to do so.

God can take burdens from us instantaneously if He chooses. Oh, how I prayed that He would! I so wanted to be changed, but I didn't want to do the work myself. I just wanted God to fix it all for me. But He had a different plan.

Instead of evaporating my depression and anxiety, He slowly taught me how to overcome them daily by depending on His strength, leaning on His grace, and trusting in His wisdom. The Scriptures are true. Perfect love really does cast out fear.

Before, I knew it as a verse. Now I own it as reality.

When I grasp how much God truly loves me (even as He performs open-heart surgery on me), the fear clawing at my guts subsides. The pain welling up within me threatening to drown me drains away. The choking despair relaxes its grip and lets hope fill my spiritual lungs with life again.

Yes, it would be easier if God would just take the hard stuff away for me, but I must admit that to feel His power surge through and around me, to lift me above the waves and propel me forward, is much more invigorating. It's truly empowering to experience firsthand what God can do through hearts that finally and fully surrender to Him.

He always comes with good and prosperous plans for me. How often I reject His gifts because I don't like the way He wrapped them. How foolish I am to refuse His ways because they seem too hard or uncomfortable or eccentric for me.

The paradox is that our greatest victory lies in our unconditional surrender. I have learned that when I resist God, I fight against my own best interest.

I never want to surrender to doubt or fear, depression or anxiety, selfishness or pride. That kind of giving-up surrender never leads to green pastures or good places. But to surrender wholly and completely to the One who loved me so much that He didn't want Heaven to be without me is a joy, not a burden.

There is still pain, but now I allow God to comfort me. There is still grief, but now I have a firm grip on hope. There are still fears that lurk ominously in the shadows, but now I have learned to rest in the loving embrace of the One who will never let me go.

Wrecked for Good

Today I rejoice that God has lifted me up out of that slimy suffocating pit and set my feet on the solid Rock of His undying love and unrelenting faithfulness. It has not been quick or easy.

My battle back to the light has been a long, difficult journey, and there are still plenty of hard days when I fumble and fall short, but the foundation of my faith is stronger than before. My experience rocked me to my core and forced me to realize I had built my faith on the ungrounded foundation of God staying predictable, answering my prayers the way I thought He should, and rewarding me immediately for my obedience.

Instead, my faith is now being built on the fact that God is exactly who He says He is every day, in every circumstance, whether I can feel it or not and whether I understand what He's doing or not.

I didn't recognize God's gifts at the time because they often come wrapped in unexpected ways, much like a Mighty Savior who came to us wrapped in a baby blanket. God is the Master of the unexpected miracle.

We often find what we seek. If we look for reasons to distrust God and doubt His love or make excuses for our disobedience, we will probably find plenty. The reverse is equally true. When we look for the beauty in our mess, the peace in our chaos, the joy in our journey, the purpose in our pain, and God's loving presence in our lives—we will find it (Matthew 7:7).

When I lost my son, I was utterly wrecked. I thought my pain was unredeemable and my life would be undone forever. Now I can see that breath-taking blossoms have gradually grown up from the ashes of despair.

I realize that God wrecked me, not to destroy me, but to bless me. I have been wrecked for good.

Worth the Climb

Having come out the other side of trauma I thought would end me, my message to you is this: God is faithful, even when we are not.

When I was too weak to hold on to God any longer, I discovered that He still held me. Though I felt alone, He was always near. He acknowledged and saved every tear that fell from my shattered heart (Psalms 56:8, NLT).

I have a new perspective now that I have climbed further up the mountain. I haven't reached the summit yet, but in many ways, I am finally above the tree line and able to appreciate and enjoy more of the magnificent view. If you are still deeper in the valleys, let me assure you that the view is worth the effort of the climb.

As I look back across the expanse of the last ten years of my wandering, I have the advantage of a new perspective. I can see now that all the circuitous routes that challenged and frustrated me were, in fact, carving a beautiful and masterful design through the landscape of my life that only God could see at the time.

For years after my son's death, I tried to return to who I used to be, but that was impossible. I am forever changed because of his brief life. At first, I changed in awful ways—a hideous twisting of who God intended me to be. But, by God's grace, I have not stayed that way.

God has been patient and powerful with me. It has taken me years, but I can finally say with complete honesty that I am better for having a hole ripped in my heart because God has filled it with Himself.

Do You Feel Defeated?

If you do not stand firm in your faith, you will not stand at all.
~ Isaiah 7:9b, NIV

Perhaps today you are in a shadowy valley yourself. Your story is different from mine, but our deepest human struggles and questions are strikingly similar no matter who we are or what shape the outer storm takes. We don't all walk through the same shadows, but we all have our valleys. We don't all break in the same places, but we all break somewhere.

Maybe you can't see where this awful road you're walking will take you. Do you feel like you're wandering aimlessly, lost without a Guide to bring you back home? Is your faith fragile, your peace tattered, and your hope frayed? Does true joy seem to be a distant and fading memory, or perhaps a misty dream that never really existed?

Do you feel beaten down and beaten up, but you can't even see who's throwing the punches at you? You know God has promised victory, but it just feels so far from what you're experiencing. You want to believe that everything God says is true and right, but your experience just doesn't seem to line up with the God you thought you knew.

The apparent unwavering faith of others only adds to your isolation. Fear of their reaction if you told them what you really think, keeps you silent and alone. You try to smother the doubts with the outward actions of a faith-filled life, but they don't go away—not completely. You feel like a hypocrite, going through the motions of devotion but feeling devoid of even a mustard seed of faith.

Hold On

I've been in that place. It's miserable. As one who is maybe a little further along the path through the valley and up the mountain than you are, I am drawn to turn back for you. I pray for you. I long to come alongside you—to sit down in the muck and the mire with you, to hold you, and to hear you, because every person's pain needs a voice.

I want you to know you are never alone and that God is always good. I am compelled to encourage you to keep believing and trusting God anyway, even when He doesn't make sense. (Because how could an infinite God ever make sense to a finite mind?)

I don't have all the answers, but I walk with the One who does. In His wisdom, He only shares what we need to know when we need to know it.

I can't fix it. I can't mend broken hearts. There is so much I am powerless to do in the face of human suffering. But if I can at least offer my companionship and share my trials and triumphs with you, then maybe we can do this thing called Life together with Jesus and come through victorious despite our suffering and setbacks. If I can ease your burden even the tiniest bit or turn your eyes to the God who sees you as His beloved treasure, then my pain will not have been in vain.

Life is a Battle, Not a Playground

> *God is strong, and he wants you strong. So take everything the*
> *Master has set out for you, well-made weapons of the best materials.*
> *And put them to use so you will be able to stand up to everything the*
> *Devil throws your way. This is no afternoon athletic contest that we'll*
> *walk away from and forget about in a couple of hours. This is*
> *for keeps, a life-or-death fight to the finish against*
> *the Devil and all his angels.*
> *~ Ephesians 6:10-12, MSG*

More than likely, you feel defeated because you're in a battle but don't know it. The world wants us to believe life's a playground. It's all about me and what makes me happy and brings me pleasure.

As we will see, Satan is behind these worldly lies. He is forever scheming to mesmerize us with entertainment, fill our bellies, distract our eyes, focus our thoughts on ourselves, and forget to keep Jesus at the center.

It may be that you don't know what enemy you are up against, what he wants, how to protect yourself, who's got your back, and what weapons, tools, and equipment are available to you or how to use them. You've forgotten or never learned that God is unbeatable and He loves you and fights for you.

It's possible you're so focused on your daily battle you forget the war is already won. You don't know who you are and that you are meant to be an overcomer, a beacon, a rescuer, a healing force of God's love in a broken world.

God's word tells us this life here and now is a battlefield. It's no accident that your world gets rocked. There is a real enemy waging a real war against your soul. You will not make it through life unscathed by the devil's attacks. It is much better to learn how to stand strong against them than to ignore them and hope they just go away.

We ignore the war raging against us to our peril. It is time to open our eyes to the devil's schemes and determine to resist him and surrender to God instead. Only then can we live the victorious and undefeated life we were meant to live.

Don't Quit

You probably picked this book up because you are feeling shaken and you want to know that victory is possible. You want to learn how you can live undefeated instead of being kicked around by an enemy you can't see.

Or you may not be in a trial now, but you know you will be eventually, because "people are born for trouble as readily as sparks fly up from a fire" (Job 5:7). Learning truths about the nature of humanity's struggle ahead of time will save you needless pain and aimless wandering.

This book will also better equip you to help someone you care about who is faltering in their faith. Rather than judging them for floundering, side-stepping their questions, or glossing over their suffering, you will be able to come alongside them with encouragement and comfort.

Even if you haven't personally wrestled with similar issues, you can understand their point of view and appreciate their doubts. You will be better able to give them space to ask the hard questions while being comfortable not knowing all the answers.

How many people abandon their faith because life didn't turn out the way they expected? How many folks quit on God because they were disillusioned when He didn't respond the way they thought He would, and disappointed when He didn't seem to show up in time?

Many who say they don't believe in God are often people who gave up on God because of unexplained suffering and unanswered questions. They are unable to find a satisfying response to the age-old question, "Why would a perfectly good God allow so much pain when He possesses the power to stop it?" And they decide a God who would allow such a thing can't possibly be worth listening to.

Take the First Step Now

You don't have to keep plugging away at life feeling beat up and defeated. It won't be quick or easy, but you can take the first steps of your journey right now. I don't want you to stay stuck for far too long as I did.

You *can* walk in victory. You just need to learn how.

When Jesus healed the lame man at the Pool of Bethesda, He instructed him to get up, pick up his mat, and claim his healing by walking it out (John 5:8). If you've been lying on your mat because you don't possess the strength or knowledge to rise, may I just hold your hand and encourage you to get up and start walking in victory now?

As Lao Tzu astutely observed, "The journey of a thousand miles begins with one step." You don't need to be overwhelmed by the whole Road to Triumph. Just take the first step of learning to stand strong in your faith and live undefeated.

Do you remember how you felt seeing your toddler poised to take that first step? That's how Jesus feels about us. Jesus celebrates our baby steps.

When your child took a tumble, what did you do? Jesus does the same. When we mess up, Jesus isn't spring-loaded to sternly scold us for not getting it right. He's eager to celebrate our growth and progress, and wrap us in warm hugs of encouragement.

He's not focused on our fall. He's full of joy at the steps we took before the fall, and He's anticipating the steps He knows we'll take next after we get back up.

Jesus offers a victorious life with your name on it. What are you waiting for? Let's get started!

CHAPTER 2

SHAKEN: WHEN FAITH FALTERS

Asking Unanswerable Questions

*"Faith does not eliminate questions. But faith knows
where to take them."*
~ Elisabeth Elliot

Do You Wonder?

Has observing God's work in this world ever left you scratching your head, wondering what He's up to? Have you ever been discouraged because God didn't come through the way you thought He would? When you witness senseless suffering, are you tempted to wonder if God has abdicated His throne?

I have. It's very uncomfortable. There have been times when I felt like the little girl in Hans Christian Andersen's story who felt compelled to say, "Umm . . . It looks to me like the Emperor isn't actually wearing any clothes."

That sounds and feels distastefully disrespectful and downright blasphemous. But as a Bible-believing, bought-by-His-blood, redeemed Christian, I have honestly thought that a time or two.

I didn't admit that out loud, of course, but that was what my heart and mind were battling when my faith collided with reality. As I tried to reconcile my shining faith with my darkened experiences, the grand promises of the Bible appeared to come up short.

God in the Hands of an Angry Sinner

How long, Lord? Will you forget me forever? How long will you hide
your face from me? How long must I wrestle with my thoughts and
day after day have sorrow in my heart? How long will
my enemy triumph over me?
~ Psalm 13:1-2, NIV

Years ago, I was taking a Counseling Practicum class while working
toward a Master's Degree in Counseling. Several times throughout
the course, our teacher showed us documentaries and mini biog-
raphies about people who had traveled unbelievably tragic and
heart-wrenching journeys. It was difficult to watch people who had
endured so much pain struggle toward wholeness for their souls.

The videos she shared covered a wide variety of topics, but there
happened to be one common thread that ran through each broken person's story—unspeakable trauma from staggeringly horrific
past child abuse. Each night after witnessing one of these videos, I
would return home disturbed and upset, aching for lost innocence
that could never be regained.

More than once, I raised my clenched fist and angry eyes toward
Heaven and accused, "How could You? How could You just sit in
Heaven with the knowledge this horror is going on, possessing the
power to stop it and yet doing nothing?"

I'm not the first to ask why an all-knowing, all-powerful,
all-loving God has not intervened, and I won't be the last. For weeks,
the only response I sensed from God was silence. Was He speechless
because He was guilty? Had I been the one after all this time to
catch Him in the act of being an unjust God?

Or was He simply ignoring me for daring to think, much less
utter, such blasphemy? Maybe my insolent questions didn't deserve
an answer. Perhaps He was just displaying mercy and restraint by not
igniting my room with a lightning bolt meant just for me.

But then, one black night, as I paced angrily in my home and
pouted about the unfairness of this sovereign God I had dared to
trust, my soul felt a tender reply. I didn't sense any anger or rejection,
just a gentle answer to soothe my frayed heart and mind.

"I love those suffering children far more than you are capable of loving anyone. I know them each by name. I know every hair on their heads. I save every tear they weep. I bear witness to every unspeakable act carried out in secrecy.

And I also love the people you cannot. I love the brutal people who committed these despicable offenses. I created them too, and I value them and refuse to violate their autonomy.

I gifted people with free will, knowing they would hurt each other and grieve My heart. But love cannot exist where there is no freedom. People must freely choose love. And I desire love above all else.

I didn't intervene the way you would have because I don't think the way you do. My thoughts are much higher, and My ways are unsearchable. That's why I call you to trust Me, and not rely on your own understanding.

You cannot fathom how, but My response is always the most loving response. I see. I know. I am mighty. I am love. It is out of love, not indifference, that I stay my hand. Trust Me, my child."

There have only been a handful of times in my life when I was sure I heard God speaking clearly and directly to my heart and mind. I knew I did not possess the capacity to create a thought like the one I just had. It was so completely different than anything I could have anticipated or expected.

My protests surrendered to His wisdom in silence. Angry thoughts quit racing through my mind. My heart warmed with the tender touch of a Love too powerful to deny.

I learned not only of the unfathomable depth of God's love for His people but also that God is big enough to handle our tough questions. We are incapable of asking something that will surprise or shock Him.

He is too smart to be caught off-guard, and too secure in Himself to feel threatened or defensive. He's too loving to be rude and too patient to write us off.

He doesn't always answer so clearly, and often, He doesn't choose to answer at all. He owes us no explanation of Himself. He has no obligation to check His plans with us and get our approval.

Any tidbits He does choose to share are bonus benefits, but we must not require answers from Him in exchange for our faith. That's not how it works. Faith must come first. Answers **may** come later.

God knows we have questions, and He permits us to ask them. God wants honest, open communication with us. He already knows our hearts and minds better than we do. We can't hide anything from Him. We might as well bring all our junk and hang-ups to Him, so He can help us sort it all out.

Other people may try to hush us up because our questions make them squirm, but God is never uncomfortable with our questions. People who are insecure about themselves don't like to be questioned. They are afraid their inadequacies will be exposed.

> God is neither insecure nor inadequate. He is big enough to handle our questions without getting ruffled.

God is neither insecure nor inadequate. He is big enough to handle our questions without getting ruffled.

We think we want answers to our questions, but what we truly need is more love. Sometimes, God withholds the answers we think we want and gives us Himself instead. He is all the answer we need.

The beauty is that when we have God Himself, we no longer need to have the answers. When we are full of His love, there is no room for anger, doubt, or fear. As He fills us with more and more of Himself, His presence drives out all others (1 John 4:18).

Not All Questions Are Created Equal

"Never doubt that there are two kinds of doubt: one that fully lives into the questions, and one that uses the questions as weapons against fully living."
~ *Ann Voskamp,* The Greatest Gift

When we question God, we generally fall into one of two camps based on the attitude of our heart. We are either seeking to understand God better or dismissing Him in mockery.

Curious Questions Seek God

Are you the Messiah we've been expecting, or should
we keep looking for someone else?
~ Luke 7:19, NLT

Curious questions are those whispered respectfully from a confused heart that desires to understand better.

When we have a seeking heart, we truly want to know and love God. We want it all to be true, but our experience isn't lining up with our understanding of who God is and how He works, and that trips us up. We are stumbling over our inability to comprehend, and so we ask God questions about who He is and what His promises mean in order to have closer fellowship with Him.

We may be impatient, skeptical, exasperated, or even rude with our questions, but that doesn't necessarily mean we are mocking God. We are just hurt, confused, and disappointed, and we want it all to make sense.

I believe John the Baptist had a seeking heart. When he asked if Jesus was the Real Deal or if he should go somewhere else, I don't think there was a hint of mockery in him. I think he was sincerely seeking to find out if he had misunderstood, because he found himself in a place he didn't expect to be—prison (Matthew 11:3).

When we are genuinely seeking the truth, boldly and openly bringing our questions to God is never wrong. Even if we, like Nicodemus, must come to Him "at night" for fear of what our peers might think of us, let us at least drop the pretense of certainty before God (John 3:1-2). He knows we are blind, stumbling in darkness until He illuminates our hearts with His truth.

Contentious Questions Mock God

Woe to those who quarrel with their Maker.
~ Isaiah 45:9a, NIV

Contentious questions are those shouted tauntingly from a rebellious heart that wants to avoid responsibility to God.

Some people who question God aren't seeking to understand or draw closer to God at all. They are just using their questions as an excuse for refusing to believe. After all, if you believe in a sovereign Creator, then you are accountable to Him, right? And truthfully, the humanness in us doesn't really want to answer to a Higher Power.

So people dodge a relationship with their Maker by listing the things they don't understand rather than taking their questions to Him and leaning on His understanding. They use unknowns as an excuse to reject the truth God is trying to reveal to them. This is the sign of a heart hardened toward God.

Flawed Motives for Questions

The Bible also includes numerous examples of questions asked from rebellious hearts. Let's take a look at how God responds to these.

Testing the Lord

The Israelites had their share of questions for God. Shortly following the most dramatic jailbreak in history overflowing with miraculous protection and provision, the Israelites started fussing about their living conditions. They got so disillusioned, they asked, "Is the Lord among us or not?" (Exodus 17:7).

The witnesses of the most spectacular sea voyage of all time now questioned whether God was even with them at all. Folks, if they could doubt God after what they experienced, then none of us are immune. For some people, any amount of miraculous demonstration from God is not enough for them to believe.

God made it clear He wasn't happy about their questions. He considered them to be testing Him. In other words, they were demanding He prove himself to them to comfort their disbelief. (Umm, hadn't He done that already?)

Before we come down too hard on the Israelites, let's keep in mind that they were upset because they were running out of water in the middle of the desert. Not having enough food and water to give your family is a serious issue—much more dire than most of the things I get worked up about.

Attempting to Trick God

Several times, the Pharisees asked Jesus questions, not to learn from Him but to tempt and trap Him. They grilled Him on taxes, an adulterous woman, marriage after resurrection, and more in an attempt to trick Him into saying something incriminating.

Friends, never try to outwit God. It's just foolish. Matthew ends his recounting of the litany of questions and answers with this comment: "No one could say a word in reply, and from that day on no one dared to ask him any more questions." (Matthew 22:46)

Excuses to Cover Rebellion

Jesus upset quite a few people when He drove out the commerce taking place in the temple during Passover. In their indignant anger, they asked, "What authority do you have to tell us what to do?"

This question was just a distraction technique so they could avoid acknowledging the truth of their own wrongdoing. The people's real intent was to incite a debate. They were sinning, and they knew it, but they stubbornly refused to respond to the clear authority and power of Jesus (John 2:18-22).

Mocking Disbelief

At His trial, Jesus was silent before His accusers. He chose to leave their insincere questions unanswered rather than defend Himself. When they hauled Him before Pilate who had the authority to condemn or acquit Him, He still refused to take the bait.

But Jesus made no reply, not even to a single charge—
to the great amazement of the governor.
~ Matthew 27:14, NIV

Spectacle Seeking

Jesus also remained silent when Pilate sent Him to Herod. Much to Herod's dismay, Jesus made it clear He won't perform on demand or satisfy our itching desire to witness the spectacular (Luke 23:8-11).

God's not here to entertain us with a magic show. He refuses to answer to our call to perform like a circus animal.

Taunts Requesting Proof

The religious leaders of Jesus' day tried to test Him by asking Him for a sign to prove Himself. His response was, "You ask for a sign. But none will be given." (Matthew 16:1-4)

The chief priests, the teachers of the law, and the elders mocked Jesus while He hung on the cross. They taunted, "Save yourself! Come down from the cross, if you are the Son of God!" (Matthew 27:41)

They fueled the skeptics' questions who might have been asking, "How can he save others if he can't even save himself?" He could have easily done so, but instead, He chose to finish the mission for which God had sent Him.

They had no desire for a relationship with Him nor any intention of understanding who He was or investigating if His claims were true. They were making fun of the man they betrayed, accused, and condemned—flaunting their taunts to a listening crowd and publicly defaming him.

Be Respectful

As we ask questions, it is important to remember our place. Let us come before Him with an attitude of seeking His wisdom, revelation, and direction rather than blaming Him or critiquing his actions, and tearing apart His plan thinking we could do better.

As we grow and flesh out the understanding of our faith, we must also remain respectful not only to God Himself but also to people who are at a different place in their faith than we are.

Remember, He is God and you are not. Question, don't quarrel. Don't be the lump of clay that fusses like a toddler at The Potter.

Two Paths

There are two paths available to us in light of the incomprehensible. We can stay stuck in a place where we can't get past our questions, falling into doubt and distrust. Or, we can choose to trust and obey Him anyway and allow the unexplainable to lead us to a place of awe and worship.

Allow your questions to lead you deeper into His presence and not further away. This is certainly the less traveled path, but it will make all the difference.

The Question of Suffering

"Satan has no more effective weapon in his arsenal than to make us question—not so much whether God exists, but whether God is really good. He knows God alone possesses the power and passion for us to be restored after being shredded in life's killing fields. For Satan to talk us into distrusting God and distancing ourselves from Him is to keep us broken, ineffective, and frankly, out of his hair. Life offers no few invitations to fall into this kind of distrust."
~ Beth Moore

How do we reconcile human suffering with a God who is purely good and completely powerful?

Why does an all-good and all-powerful God allow his people to suffer?

These are age-old questions that people have asked through the centuries. I imagine the first person to ask it might have been Eve when one of her sons murdered another. These questions keep coming up because suffering is prevalent, complicated, and difficult. Truly satisfying answers are scarce.

The Question of Suffering applies in this context because we are apt to ask some variant of this when we are feeling defeated and vulnerable. It's so easy to wonder, "Where's God now?", especially when we have trusted Him and fully expected Him to show up in power in the middle of our mess.

It is so common to wonder about these things. Yet, there are not many places among Christian circles where people feel "safe" asking the big questions about God. But I know it is far better to ask your questions and wrestle with possible answers than to walk away from God altogether in disappointment, confusion, and bitterness.

So let's take a closer look at these three questions.

1. What causes human suffering?
2. Why does God allow us to suffer?
3. How should we respond to suffering?

As you read the rest of this chapter, ask yourself, "How does the way I answer these questions change the way I live my day-to-day life?" Theology is only beneficial to the degree that we live it out practically.

1. What causes human suffering?

Usually, the vast majority of human suffering falls into one of four categories. We suffer as a result of:

- Our own poor choices
- Ungodly decisions of others
- Natural consequences of living in a post-paradise world
- Because we're exactly where God wants us to be

Our Own Sin

Sometimes we suffer as a result of our own sin. Just as there are physical laws that govern our existence, there are spiritual laws as well. If I were to attempt to live my life as if there is no gravity, I would be a fool—a severely injured fool.

One spiritual law is the Law of Sowing and Reaping. You reap what you sow. In the physical world, if I plant watermelon seeds and expect to harvest tomatoes, I am a fool.

Similarly, if I sow behaviors in my life that are inconsistent with how God calls me to live and yet I still expect to reap the rewards of a life well-lived, I am also a fool. If I plant sin, I will harvest suffering as sure as gravity will pull me down when I jump.

A Biblical example of this type of suffering is the first king of Israel. King Saul disobeyed God's commands to him on numerous occasions. As a result, he lost the throne, and even more painfully, God's favor upon his life.

He suffered from fits of rage and tried to kill his loyal servant and future king of Israel, David. Saul's suffering was completely avoidable and unnecessary if only he had done what God asked of him.

We must tread carefully here. The Church has a notorious history of linking suffering and sin incorrectly. We can never assume that suffering is the result of sin. It may be, but we cannot play God in this matter.

We can also make the mistake of thinking we are innocent when we are not. Be brave enough to ask God to show you where you are creating or contributing to your own trouble. He'll probably be kind enough to point it out to you.

We must be careful not to err in falsely accusing others of sin they didn't commit nor incorrectly acquitting ourselves of sins we *did* commit. Neither error puts the sufferer on the path to wholeness.

Someone Else's Sin

There are numerous times throughout our lives when we are hurt, directly or indirectly, by the sin of another person. God doesn't violate anybody's free will. The option to follow or disregard His commands is up to each one of us.

Sin always has rippling effects that radiate out with all sorts of unintended consequences. Not because God is punishing us, but because willfully stepping out of bounds opens us and our loved ones up to all kinds of suffering from which God would prefer to spare us. You only have to catch a tiny glimpse of today's news to see horrific examples of this type of suffering all over the place.

In the Bible, Joseph's brothers sold him into slavery. Then he was accused of a crime he didn't commit and thrown in jail. He was forgotten and left to rot there until somebody remembered he was useful.

Throughout these unjust ordeals, Joseph remained faithful to God and continued to try to do the right thing. His suffering was largely the result of other people's sins rather than his own.

Now, just because another person has sinned against us, does not make us totally innocent. Very often, we suffer for both of the above reasons at the same time. This is especially true in our relationships with others. Rarely is one party completely innocent and the other totally guilty. Even so, the other people in our most difficult relationships are not our true enemies. We'll talk more about this in Chapter 5.

Living in a Fallen World

The world we live in now is not the paradise it was created to be, nor the glory it will be one day. Sadly, sin has distorted our physical world as much as it has our spiritual world.

There are natural consequences that come with living in a fallen world. We grow old. Our bodies fail. Viruses that are too small for us to see attack and overtake us. Hurricanes, flood, earthquakes, droughts, and fires claim innocent lives. These are not the results of any particular person's sin, but just because we live in a sin-polluted world that is not immune from the effects of spiritual rebellion.

The incredibly Good News is that one day, God will make everything right again—both in creation and in our frail earthly bodies (Romans 8:18-25). He is hinting at that marvelous transformation even now.

Because We Obey

Most perplexing of all is the fact that sometimes we suffer *because* we obey and we are in the middle of God's will, exactly where He wants us to be.

- Job was singled out by God and harassed by Satan because he was a righteous man (Job 1:8-12).

- Joseph got thrown in jail for refusing to have another man's wife (Genesis 39).

- Jesus' disciples met a terrifying storm on the sea because they got in the boat just as He told them to (Mark 4:35-41).

- Paul was imprisoned, flogged, beaten, stoned, shipwrecked and more (2 Corinthians 11:25-27) because he was doing exactly what God wanted him to do, which was to tell the Jews, Gentiles, and kings about the resurrection of Christ (Acts 9:15-16).

- One of the hardest parts about losing my son Timothy was the fact that I was only pregnant to begin with because I had obeyed. I had to surrender my own will to allow this child to grow in my womb in the first place. Then, I had to release everything all over again to give him back to God. This back-to-back double surrender of the same child greatly contributed to me becoming undone.

- Of course, we must always look to Jesus Himself. No one on earth ever was or ever will be more sinless or purer than Jesus. And yet, no one ever has or ever will suffer to the extent that He did. No one else will ever carry the sins of all of humanity. Jesus asked for another way, but He still submitted to God's plan (Luke 22:42).

We can only see our pain and the mess we're stuck in. God can see all the beauty that will grow out of those ashes. Sometimes our life feels like a compost heap—dead, rotting, and stinky. But it's that very season of death that nurtures the new life that is to come.

Just as dead organic material produces good compost that enriches the soil and nourishes the plants which become our food, our suffering can produce within us the richness of God that nourishes our soul and one day enables us to comfort others (2 Corinthians 1:3-4).

In the end. . .

- Job and his companions had a whole new appreciation for who God is. God stretched their understanding of Him as they wrestled with His reasons for allowing Job to suffer. Then

God restored everything that Job had lost and more (Job 42:10-13).

- Joseph became ruler of Egypt, second only to Pharaoh, and was reunited with his family (Genesis 41:41-44). He rescued the nation from starvation during an extreme famine.

- Jesus' disciples got a front row seat to an unbelievable miracle that left them asking, "Who is this? Even the wind and waves obey Him!" (Mark 4:41).

- Paul carried the Good News of God's redemption of man to most of the known world and wrote roughly one-third of the New Testament.

- I have learned that God's mysterious ways are far better than I can imagine and that everything I have is a precious gift from Him.

- And Jesus bought our very lives with His own blood. (Galations 3:13-14, Revelation 5:9)

Clearly, God has His purposes in even the most perplexing pain He allows. Which leads us to our next question.

2. Why does God allow us to suffer?

Human suffering and tragedy would be easier to swallow if God did not claim to be all-powerful. Maybe He would like to help us but is just not strong enough to hold back evil and disaster.

Or perhaps if God were not all-good, we could make sense of it. If He behaved more like a selfish, immature human (such as the Greco-Roman gods were wont to do), then our seemingly random pain wouldn't need to be explained. God was just in a bad mood or being a jerk that day.

The trouble comes when we try to reconcile an all-powerful, all-loving God with the vastness of human hurt we experience and witness. This is especially true when innocents, children, and people who have made good choices suffer seemingly arbitrarily. Why does God allow this?

Entire books have been written trying to answer this question. I don't understand it all, and I can't begin to unpack it all here. This I do know: God always has a purpose in the pain He allows. He wastes nothing. He is not capricious or cruel, arbitrary or apathetic. Neither is He powerless to hold back human suffering.

> God always has a purpose in the pain He allows. He wastes nothing. He is not capricious or cruel, arbitrary or apathetic.

There's a Purpose in the Pain

Everything that He allows to touch our lives happens for a reason—for our good and His glory. Sometimes we get to see the reason later on in life. Many times, we don't.

Here is a partial list of a few of the purposes God has in our pain that will help get you started in considering some of the good God produces through our suffering.

- Our personal and spiritual growth often accelerates during times of difficulty.

- Our limitations and problems keep us aware of our dependence on Him.

- We are often more aware of the presence of God when we hurt.

- Our faith and character are refined through trials (if we are willing to allow it).

- Sometimes, what seems cruel and awful is actually God lovingly shielding us from something much worse we can't perceive or even imagine.

- Often, our trials set the stage for something better that wouldn't have happened otherwise.

- We share in Christ's sufferings now to share His glory later. (Romans 8:17, 1 Peter 4:13)

- We have greater compassion for others who are hurting.

- Common sorrows unite us with people we may not have ever talked to otherwise.

- Through our struggles we learn that our true strength comes from God alone.

- God is glorified when others witness the way He sustains and strengthens us.

- God is the world's greatest Storyteller. Stories without conflict are dull and lifeless.

This is truly a tiny and inadequate list. I cover God's purposes and promises much more in depth in Book Three of the Stand Strong series, *UNSHAKABLE: Stand Strong Even When Your World Gets Rocked.*

God has infinitely more purposes going on "behind the scenes." We will not always be able to discern what they are, but we can rest knowing that He has good purposes for us even if He chooses not to reveal them in this lifetime.

3. How should we respond to suffering?

God has good intentions toward us even in our most painful suffering, but our enemy loves to use our pain to distort our thinking about God. When we suffer, we are vulnerable to the lies he whispers that sound like our own thoughts.

God has promised He will never leave us and no one can snatch us from His hands (Deuteronomy 31:6, John 10:28). Satan can't beat us there. But if Satan can lie and make us think God has abandoned us, he might be able to convince us to walk away from God. And all too many people take him up on that offer.

So we must be bold and do the opposite. We must respectfully take our questions to God and lay them out before Him to seek His counsel. We must create safe places to wrestle with hard questions as we allow ourselves and our friends to search for God without freaking out on them.

When I find myself asking the unanswerable questions, I often change my question to, "Lord, what do you want me to learn from this?" Rather than wasting my life away chasing down mysteries not meant for me, it helps to focus my energy on what I *can* learn.

Applying God's wisdom to my life through obedient action is a much more productive way to suffer than getting stuck going round and round in the same whirlpool of swirling questions. I am learning to allow the pressure of my pain to push me closer to God rather than pull me further away in disappointment and bitterness.

In all his unfair suffering, Job never blamed God. He voiced his questions for God, but never got answers. God gave a beautiful, inspiring, compassionate, and humbling response to Job, but He didn't explain Himself.

Job's response was, "Surely I spoke of things I did not understand, things too wonderful for me to know." (Job 42:3b) In the end, God praised Job for being honest (Job 42:8). God doesn't owe us any answers, but He doesn't mind us bringing Him our questions.

Philip Yancey pointed out in his book, *Where Is God When It Hurts?*, "We never know in advance exactly how suffering can be transformed into a cause for celebration. But that is what we are asked to believe. Faith means believing in advance what will only make sense in reverse."

In the end, it comes back around to faith. Our faith in God is built on a foundation of trust. We will examine more reasons and ways to trust God in Chapter 8.

Blurry Vision

> We don't yet see things clearly. We're squinting in a fog, peering
> through a mist. But it won't be long before the weather clears and
> the sun shines bright! We'll see it all then, see it all as clearly as God
> sees us, knowing him directly just as he knows us! But for right now,
> until that completeness, we have three things to do to lead us toward
> that consummation: Trust steadily in God, hope unswervingly, love
> extravagantly. And the best of the three is love.
> ~ 1 Corinthians 13:12-13, MSG

We are human, so we will have questions. God has revealed many wonderful truths to us, but many of our questions will go unanswered this side of Heaven, and we have to learn to be okay with that. We see dimly and partially now, but one day, we will see all things clearly.

Until we have complete knowledge and understanding, we must learn to live with the tension of a fuzzy vantage point while we rely on faith, hope, and love to see us through. All three of these essentials are gifts from God, and when we separate ourselves from Him because we are confused, we reject the source of healing for our pain. We spit in the face of the Physician who is trying to mend our brokenness.

Over the past few years, there have been many times when I wrestled with God and sought answers to the hard questions. I know I'm not the only one. More Christians and would-be Christians wrestle over how to reconcile their pain with God's complete sovereignty and goodness than many of us would like to admit. I used to be a closet questioner, but not anymore. I want to be open about my questions but not let the unanswered questions weaken my trust in God.

In addition to asking questions, sometimes we find ourselves wondering if God is really who He says He is and if we can really trust His promises. Sometimes, faith gets complicated and confusing. What do we do with our doubts? Does it mean we're a weak Christian if we wrestle with the unknowns?

CHAPTER 3

DOUBTING: WHEN FAITH GETS CONFUSING

Overcoming Uncertainty

"I do not believe there ever existed a Christian yet, who did not now and then doubt his interest in Jesus. I think, when a man says, 'I never doubt,' it is quite time for us to doubt him."
~ Charles Spurgeon

Where is Your God Now?

It's easy to trust God when we feel secure and we know He's got our back and we have His blessings. But when we can't find Him in the dark storm that is raging around us, we quickly become undone.

Doubts threaten to overwhelm our faith, and questions push aside our confidence. What once was secure is now shaken, and we're not sure how to respond when a watching world mocks, "Where is your God now?"

The Doubting Thomas of Christmas

I don't remember a time I believed in Santa Claus. I was the Doubting Thomas of Christmas. My scientific mind knew it was impossible for one man and a handful of reindeer to traverse the globe in a single night.

Every year, I tried to stay up and "catch him in the act." (Or catch my parents rather, who I assumed were behind the whole charade.) I would question my mom about how Santa could be in two different malls at once and dismiss her explanation of his helpful elves that fill in for him during the busy month of December.

I will never forget the magical Christmas at my grandmother's house, when all the grandkids were awoken in the middle of the night to our parents excitedly proclaiming, "He's here! Wake up, kids! He's here!" We rushed from our bedrooms into the large dining and living area, and sure enough, there was Santa Claus with his bag and the gifts and even the "Ho ho ho!"

I wondered if maybe I had been wrong...until I caught a brief glimpse of the tuft of dark brown hair sticking out from under his wig. "Aha! I caught you, Santa. You're the fake I always thought you were." I went back to bed tired from all the excitement, holding my new doll, with the smug little smile of a satisfied detective.

Sadly, I did the same thing to God, approaching Him as though He was a mythical Santa figure who must prove his existence to me. I stood before Him, my arms across my chest, and cross-examined His testimony about His past miracles and future promises.

I scoffed at the miraculous as if His works were as preposterous as flying reindeer. What I didn't understand, I rejected. Because if I couldn't grasp it, how could it possibly be true?

I expected to find proof any moment that it was just a wig, or to discover the emperor wasn't wearing fancy finery but leading a parade in his underwear. I wondered if someday I will watch as a yippy dog pulls back the curtain and reveals the "wizard" for what he is—the imagination of some misplaced, misguided, desperate soul trying to make the best of a tough situation.

Isolated by Doubt

"Belief in God does not exempt us from feelings of abandonment by God. Praising God does not inoculate us from doubts about God."
~ Eugene Peterson

Too often, life kicks us in the gut, and we doubt beliefs that are much more significant and fundamental than a man in a red suit. Forget Santa. I need to know if God is real and if He cares, not just in a general sense, but does He care about *me* and the matters that concern those I care about personally.

When God took my baby in such a sudden and traumatic way, it sucked the wind out from under my wings, sending me into a tailspin. Uncertainty swirled around me, pulling me downward into a spiral of faithless questions and doubtful declarations. I was terribly confused.

It seemed I was suffering **because** I obeyed, and that threw me for a nasty loop. If I get slammed for doing my best to follow what I believed God told me, what does that say about His character? Where is the goodness and mercy in that?

I was devastated. I felt betrayed, hurt, and terribly disappointed—not just disappointed in myself or how my life had turned out, but deeply disappointed in God. He hadn't shown up the way I thought He would, which I incorrectly interpreted as deliberate neglect.

That was bad, but what was worse was that I had no safe place to wonder aloud or talk through my doubts and confusion. It somehow felt blasphemous to breach the topic of God's apparent unfairness and cruelty. What would my Christian friends think of me if I told them what I was actually thinking? I didn't bother to find out.

Isolated and alone in my prison of doubt, I was too proud to talk with other Christians and too angry to talk to God. I couldn't seem to pull myself together spiritually, and so I added self-condemnation to the pile of burdens I was never meant to carry. What was one more boulder when I was already crushed, right?

Other Christians didn't seem to wrestle with the questions and doubts that kept me up at night. Why was my faith so much weaker than theirs? I thought of people like Corrie Ten Boom who maintained her faith and upheld the banner of love amid horrific circumstances, unimaginable cruelty, and crushing grief.

How was she able to do that? Why do I come undone with so much lesser problems? Why was it so hard for me to believe God's promises are true?

Two Types of Doubt

In wrestling through my doubts over a number of years, I have come to learn that there are different types of doubt. Either I have doubts about God because I struggle intellectually to grasp His plan, or I understand fine but I'm hesitant to act on that belief in real-life personal application.

Mental Doubts

> *Can a mortal be innocent before God? Can anyone be pure before the Creator? If God does not trust his own angels and has charged his messengers with foolishness, how much less will he trust people made of clay! They are made of dust, crushed as easily as a moth.*
> *~ Job 4:17-19, NLT*

Mental doubt occurs when my brain thinks, "This doesn't add up." I don't have enough information or understanding to make sense of what God's doing in my world. When my experience doesn't seem to mesh with who God says He is and all that He's promised, I'm left scratching my head.

I get suspicious that maybe God wasn't up front with me after all. Surely His promise that whatever I ask in His name will be granted must have some other meaning than what I thought. I've been crying out with faith and passion for what I believe is God's will, and it still seems to me like He hasn't shown up. What gives?

He told me if I ask I'd receive, and if I sought I would find, and if I knock the doors would fly open. So why do I feel empty and lost? Why does it seem He slammed the door in my face when I knocked instead of answering my plea for help? Is He for real, or have I been swindled?

As I shared already, I experienced a crisis of intellectual doubt with Santa Claus as a child. In the end, I discovered I was right. It was a sham. Would my doubts about God lead to the same end?

Children tend to believe freely, but adults have spent years building walls to protect themselves from being duped into false hope and extravagant promises that turn out to be dead ends. We launch our Triple A (AAA—Anti-Aircraft Artillery) and pierce the sky of faith with a hundred missiles of uncertainty born out of our insecurity and fear of disappointment.

The defensive measures we erect to shield ourselves from disillusionment only succeed in further isolating ourselves from God's loving presence, which provide no protection at all. We are putting ourselves at risk of playing right into the hands of the enemy who has schemed against us.

Ten out of twelve Hebrews on the recon team doubted to the point of disobedience, and they missed out on claiming the abundance and beauty God had promised them (Numbers 13). It was not God's unfaithfulness that negated the promise. They were held back because they chose to emphasize their doubts and fears over trusting God to make good on the promise.

Willful Doubts

There is a second type of doubt that does not so much involve our intellectual assertions as it does our real-life application of those professions. We may say

> Faith is belief put into action.

we believe one thing, but then we live like it's not true. How often I have caught myself doing this very thing!

This is the kind of faith that says the ice is thick enough to walk across but always walks around the lake just in case. It's one thing for me to say I believe the bungee cord is strong enough to hold me, but it is another thing entirely to jump off the bridge with confidence that the cord will keep me from impacting the ground at a scary high velocity.

Faith is belief put into action. If I say I believe something is true, but I never have enough confidence to act on it, then I don't have the faith I claim to have in that belief.

We deceive ourselves when we claim to have faith in God and then act like it's all up to us to get the job done. This too is doubt. Intellectually, we may be on board with Jesus, but until we step out of the boat in faith upon the waters, we're just cowardly doubters. We believe, but not enough to bet our lives on it.

Peter did it. He got out of the boat. His only Life Preserver was the Son of God. He didn't pack his PFD (Personal Flotation Device) just in case Jesus wasn't at the top of His game that day.

Peter just stood up and stepped out, trusting in God more than his understanding of physics.

But here's the part that cracks me up every time I read it. Peter checked out the wind and the waves, and then backed down. (Because everyone knows walking on waves is *so much* harder than just walking on a flat sea! You're already doing the impossible, dude! Just keep going!)

Apparently, Peter believed the waves were just a bridge too far for Jesus to overcome. Yet, one is just as impossibly difficult as the other!

It's easy for me to sit in my comfy chair on dry land and ridicule poor Peter, but the part that makes me uncomfortable is that I'm just as guilty of setting limits on what I believe God can do.

My head understands the concept that nothing is impossible for God. All tasks are easy for an unlimited and all-powerful God to accomplish. But in practice, I act like there are some things He is impotent to do.

I believe God is omnipresent, and yet I often act like I'm alone and abandoned.

I believe God knows everything, and yet I feel the need to inform Him about what's going on in my life and what I think He should do about it.

I believe God is the Almighty All-Powerful One, and yet I can't see how He could fix the mess I'm in. I mean, it's hopeless, right?

I believe God's plans are better than mine, but I 'm attached to the plans I thought up myself, and I have trouble laying them down. Can't He just hear me out? Maybe I thought of something He overlooked.

Peter allowed his circumstances to overrule what he believed to be true about Jesus, and it affected his actions. The result was a desperate plunge into the sea and a panicked flail to reach for rescue from the very One he had doubted.

I'm often in the same boat, or rather, flailing desperately in the same waves with Peter because I too allow my experience to eclipse my faith. What about you? Are you in the water with us or looking down on us smugly while you stroll across the sea?

Whether our doubt manifests in our minds or our will, it doesn't surprise or offend God. He knows our internal struggles even more intimately than we do.

What Do We Do with Our Doubt?

*"The minute we begin to think we know all the answers, we forget
the questions, and we become smug like the Pharisee who listed all
his considerable virtues, and thanked God that he was not like other
men... Those who believe they believe in God, but without passion
in the heart, without anguish of mind, without uncertainty, without
doubt, and even at times without despair, believe only in the
idea of God, and not in God himself."*
~ Madeleine L'Engle

Doubts are inevitable for most of us. The more honest and intellectual we are, the more so. Though doubts are common, they are not comfortable.

It can be unsettling when we realize we're not sure we really believe what we claim to or that we're not willing to act on what we say we believe.

We can wear ourselves out playing the Devil's advocate, always trying to point out where we think God has failed. Not to mention, we rob ourselves of all the joy and peace He has for us when we fail to rest our mind peacefully in His perfection.

Ignoring or denying doubt will not make it go away. I've tried that. It only left a gigantic ugly elephant in the room between God and me, and distanced me from fellow Christians who I assumed would not understand. But maybe they were hiding their doubts too. What if we had been brave enough to share our common struggle?

So, what *do* we do with our doubt? There are four steps we can take to overcome and diminish our doubt.

1. **ACCEPT** that doubt is a fact of life.

2. **EXPOSE** your doubts for what they are.

3. **SHARE** your struggles with godly people you trust.

4. **SURRENDER** your uncertainty to a trustworthy God.

ACCEPT

The strain of doubt is very uncomfortable for us, especially when our doubt swirls around God's character and plans. It feels so unholy to have questions about God, and some Christians mistakenly label *all* questions as blasphemy.

Don't fret or beat yourself up about it. Having doubts does not mean you are an inferior Christian, just a thinking one. Learn to be okay living with the tension of unanswerable questions.

Only God has all the answers. The rest of us will be trying to figure it out until the day we die, so let's just get real and admit that now.

He is the great God of mysteries. He keeps some things hidden on purpose until just the right time. Others He keeps from us because He knows it would be impossible for us to understand anyway. Several years ago, I decided that if God were small enough for my little finite brain to understand Him completely, then He wouldn't be worthy of my worship.

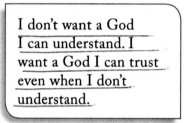

I don't want a God
I can understand. I
want a God I can trust
even when I don't
understand.

Here's the deal: I don't want a God I can understand. I want a God I can trust even when I don't understand. And God has demonstrated He is trustworthy time and time again. The life, death, and resurrection of Jesus are more than enough proof that God loves us infinitely and will pay any price to rescue us from every mess we have gotten ourselves into and every pit into which we've been pushed.

EXPOSE

- Bring your doubt into the light. No more doubt stuffing!

Doubts grow in the dark; bring them out into the light. You are not alone, and there is nothing wrong with you.

It's okay to wonder and wrestle. It's okay to not know all the answers or have everything figured out. Don't give into the pressure to pretend that you do.

It can be downright ridiculous the way we Christians try to act like we've got it all figured out. Too often, we are like the fairytale emperor, too vain to admit we don't see what others claim we should. And so we strut about in our little parade, proud yet ridiculously exposed.

Let's just be honest. Let's come right out and say that we don't have all the answers (and never will), but we know the One who does, and that's enough. This is the necessary step to dealing with our doubts and questions in a godly and productive way.

Trying to stuff your embarrassing doubt problem in the dark corners of your mind will not make it disappear nor hide it from God. Denying our doubts may let us pretend we are strong, but it only weakens our faith. It also gives the false impression of certainty to others, which causes them to also hide their doubts.

- Identify your specific doubts.

Pull the doubt clutter out of your mental closet so you can deal with it. Bring them out into the open light so you can examine them carefully. Don't just continue to own them without scrutiny.

Sometimes our doubts and assumptions are so deep-rooted that we aren't even consciously aware of them. Identify and name your doubts. Don't be afraid to ask yourself hard questions: What's the root issue? Why am I tripping on this particular idea and not others? Many times, our doubts can spring up from painful places in our lives as the unhappy result of failing to process our hurts in light of God's unchanging truths. Or we can carry on the legacy of doubt passed on to us by family, teachers, mentors, and other people we value and emulate.

- Drag your doubt to God and admit your concerns to Him.

Don't think you can work it out on your own, distancing yourself from God while you try to sort it all out. That's what I did. I'll spare you the trouble and just tell you right now that it doesn't work. Wrestling through our issues *with* God rather than wrestling *against* God makes our faith muscles grow stronger.

Jacob was known for wrestling with God. Like him, you may walk away from the wrestling match out of joint. You may never be the same again, in a good way. This type of wrestling with God forces us to depend on Him and not ourselves. Jacob had some degree of physical strength taken from him. He walked with a limp for the rest of his life. But spiritually, he was a new man with a new name—a stronger man with a bolder faith (Genesis 32:22-32).

Jesus is the Author and Perfecter of our faith (Hebrews 12:2). Our faith is the medium through which we are saved (Ephesians 2:8) and the means by which we can live a life that pleases the Lord (Hebrews 11:6). We are unable to perfect it alone. We must confront our doubts in the presence of our God if we hope to fortify our faith.

Do not fear approaching God with your wonderings and misgivings. God is not angry with you for wavering. (Even though well-meaning fellow Christians may be.) He already knows we are prone to it. He is not disappointed in us.

> God's Truth is powerful enough to withstand any assault, tight enough to survive any cross-examination, and tough enough to weather any storm.

God is bigger than your questions and mightier than your doubts. You aren't hurting His feelings. He can handle the truth. He is self-sufficient. He doesn't require our "likes" and "shares" to boost His ego. He has all He needs in and of Himself. He calls us to believe Him, not for His benefit, but for our own. He doesn't *need* us. He *wants* us—because He loves us.

Talk to him about where your faith stumbles. Let your questions lead you deeper into his presence and not further away. Our wonder should lead us to a place of praise rather than the doldrums of doubt. Press into Him. Lean on His understanding.

Let it all out. Lay all that is in your heart and your mind before the Lord. Give Him the chance to cleanse your wounds and heal your hurts. Often, our doubts are born in a broken heart. Don't let them fester and rot beneath a dirty Band-Aid. Bring yourself and all your baggage before the Great Physician. He waits ready to make you whole, not rip you apart in judgment.

Don't be afraid to push hard on His Truth. It will stand. God's Truth is powerful enough to withstand any assault, tight enough to survive any cross-examination, and tough enough to weather any storm. Don't be afraid to examine God's claims closely. Be bold to prove the truth of God's Word by living it out in spite of your uncertainties.

Ask Him to help you resolve your misgivings as you read the Bible. To be a Christian in the first place requires you to believe that God raised Jesus Christ from the dead. Belief in "lesser" miracles and mysteries should not present an insurmountable challenge once the first is embraced.

SHARE

It takes courage to question what everyone else seems to accept without a problem. Frankly, most times I haven't had the boldness to ask my questions aloud. The sad result is that I become not just confused but also painfully lonely.

Our enemy doesn't want us to take our questions to God. He wants us to turn inward with them and distance ourselves from God. He also wants us to keep separated from others who wrestle with the same questions for God, because it is in fellowship and community that our questions can be rightly examined and released.

As we reason and wrestle with God, we don't have to be alone. Doubting our faith can make us feel isolated from the very people who could help us most. God often ministers to us through the wise, godly counsel of fellow believers.

It is beneficial to reason and wrestle with life alongside other godly-minded people who are also seeking the truth. Find a safe place to share, wonder, question, and express your unique mixture of both faith and doubt. Don't be afraid to ask hard questions and seek out people who will let you give voice to them. Seek God for the answers He chooses to reveal to you.

Don't forget to become that safe place for others. Model God's unconditional love and acceptance in the face of another person's doubt and confusion. He does not silence the questioner. Why do we?

Allow yourself and others room to admit doubts without judgment. Work with others to build and nurture a Christian culture where spiritual honesty is embraced rather than scorned.

Accept the one whose faith is weak, without quarreling
over disputable matters.
~ Romans 14:1, NIV

SURRENDER

- Surrender your doubt and trade it for faith.

Even when we take our doubts to God and process through our conflicting thoughts and emotions with Him, He is not compelled to settle every matter to our liking. When we surrender our messy pain to Him, He does not necessarily box it all up with a neat bow. Questions will always remain this side of Eternity. We have to learn to be okay with that. We must let go of our desire to figure everything out. God will reveal everything we need to know, but He won't satisfy our curiosity just for the fun of it. Willingly surrender your questions to the only One who has all the answers.

I'm never as smart as I think I am or I'd like to be. At the end of the day, I have to surrender all I don't understand to the God who's already written the whole story and is both waiting at the finish line and running the race with me, cheering me on.

Faith is not something we manufacture from a satisfied intellect. Offer your doubts to Him in exchange for faith. Doubt is not the opposite of faith. Fear is the opposite of faith.

We may not understand it all clearly, but we can recount what God has done for us. We need to look no further than the cross. God did not even spare his own Son but gave Him up willingly for us. How can we *not* trust a love like *that*? Surely He means us no harm in the troubling situation we now find ourselves if He has already sacrificed His first and Best and Only for us.

Conquering circumstances with our minds will not bring peace anyway. Trusting that God has it all figured out is what brings the peace. By withholding information, we wouldn't understand any-way—He forces us to trust Him rather than foolishly rely on our weak intellect.

When we learn to live unoffended by the conundrums of the Sovereign God's interaction with willful humans, we learn to live in the blessings of God's perfect presence and peace.

- Choose victory over doubt by walking in the light of what you know.

These steps can help diminish doubt greatly, but may not make it go away altogether. That's okay. Even if all your doubts don't dissolve, you can still choose to live victoriously anyway.

There comes the point where we have to lay our doubt-wrestling aside and walk in light of the truth we already know. We will always have unanswered questions and uncertain beliefs lurking around the corners of our faith, but that should not be an excuse to keep us from acting in faith on all we do know for certain.

Let us hold unswervingly to the hope we profess,
for he who promised is faithful.
~ Hebrews 10:23, NIV

God has already revealed more than enough. We could live a hundred lifetimes and still not master the extent and application of what He's already told us. We can't sit around philosophizing, waiting for answers to all our questions and solutions to all our problems before we are willing to move forward in faith.

Don't waste too much time and effort pondering the confusing. Instead, obey the clear. Do what you know and trust God to reveal and clarify what you need to know along the way. You can take the first step without knowing what will follow or how it will all work out in the end. The next step of obedience does not depend on gaining complete understanding.

When Jesus healed the man who had been unable to walk for nearly 40 years, He didn't explain the miracle in detail. He simply instructed the man to stand up, pick up his mat, and start walking (John 5:8). Jesus told the man to do the impossible without any further clarification. Astonishingly, when the man obeyed, he found his legs were able to support him. Did it matter that he couldn't understand how? He was walking after half a lifetime of immobility!

What if the man had responded to Jesus with the argument that what he had been asked to do was impossible? What if he questioned Jesus about why his legs didn't work as well as others? What if he simply scoffed at Jesus, doubting His authority to heal, and dismissed Him as a fool?

He would have missed his miracle if he had focused on his doubts and limitations. I can imagine myself in that man's place doing those very things. I wonder how many times I have missed my miracle because my attention was on my overwhelming problems rather than on my overcoming God.

A God without Limits

Every thoughtful person has doubts about God from time to time whether they will admit it (even to themselves) or not. We can doubt by struggling to wrap our minds around a God so immense He cannot be circumscribed.

We also show our doubt when we say we believe something but are unwilling to act on it. Doubting God means you are human, not worthless. Give yourself permission to doubt and room to wrestle with life's most important questions. But always remain respectful. Remember, He's God, and we're not.

We choose victory over doubts by choosing to believe anyway, even when God doesn't make sense and even when we don't have all the answers.

CHAPTER 4

BELIEVING ANYWAY: EVEN WHEN GOD DOESN'T MAKE SENSE

Moving Beyond Unsolvable Mysteries

*"I simply do not see the bigger picture, but I **choose to believe** that there is a bigger picture and that my loss is part of some wonderful story authored by God himself."*
~ *Jerry Sittser,* A Grace Disguised

Help My Unbelief!

I identify with the desperate dad who brought his troubled son to Jesus and said, *"If you can do anything, take pity on us and help us."*

" *'If you can'?"* said Jesus. *"Everything is possible for one who believes."*

Immediately, the boy's father exclaimed, *"I do believe; help me overcome my unbelief!"* (Mark 9:22b-24, NIV)

To believe anyway, in spite of a tremendous pull to do otherwise, is the essence of faith. If everything made sense and always worked out just the way we think it should, there would be no need for faith.

We cannot wait until we make sense of it all to follow God. But we never will this side of Eternity, at least not all of it. It comes down to an issue of trust. Will you choose to trust God even when you can't figure Him out?

"No sin will ruin us but unbelief which is a sin against the remedy."
~ Matthew Henry

Above the Clouds

Our family loves to downhill ski. One very gray and cloudy morning, we drove two hours to the nearby ski slope. About halfway up the mountain, we broke through the low-lying cloud layer. The snow-covered mountains were blindingly sunny.

I looked down into the valley below where we had just been, but all I could see was thick foggy clouds covering everything. The clouds and mountain tops were the only things visible for as far as I could see.

My depression and anxiety can color the way I view my life. Sometimes I see everything in darkened shades, and there are days when all I can see are the clouds and the storms. But I try to remember that the sun is always shining above the clouds even when I can't see it.

I choose to believe it's true even when I can't see it. Perspective makes all the difference.

Often, we get so focused on our questions and doubts that we forget about the Light we do have. We have to make a deliberate decision to focus our attention on our Creator rather than our conundrums.

I do not concern myself with great matters or things too wonderful for
me. But I have calmed and quieted myself, I am like a weaned child
with its mother; like a weaned child I am content.
~ Psalm 131:1b-2, NIV

At the beginning of Psalm 131, David tells us he intentionally let go of his unanswered questions and calmed himself in God's presence. The peace David describes in this Psalm is active, purposeful, and intentional.

Spiritual rest doesn't just happen. Peace doesn't sneak up on us like some spiritual sedative while we're concentrating on freaking out. God doesn't capture us and hold us down and force us to be calm. Releasing our cloudy thinking and gloomy moods requires deliberate and purposeful action.

Nichole Nordeman is one of my favorite songwriters. She has a way of giving words to the thoughts I possess but can't quite name. In her song, "Someday," she sings, "I will still sleep peacefully, with answers out of reach for me."

As a modern psalmist, I hear her echoing David. She has deliberately chosen to calm and quiet herself in the presence of weighty questions with incomplete answers. As she rests her uncertainty on the bosom of her all-knowing, all-loving, all-powerful God, she inspires me to do the same.

We have a choice to make. Will we settle down and rest in God's power? What would life be like if we stopped trying to solve the unsolvable puzzles of life and simply moved into His sanctuary allowing His perfect peace to smooth our frayed edges and soothe our rattled nerves?

Not Meant to Know

"But faith is not 'trusting God when we understand His ways'—there is no need for faith then. Faith is trusting when nothing is explained. Faith rests under the unexplained."
~ Amy Carmichael

God often surprises and confuses us with how He interacts with us. We are mystified by His miracles, puzzled by His plans, and bewildered by His ways.

If God gave us all the answers, we'd probably take them and go our way, but He wants so much more for us. He wants to have a close, meaningful relationship with us. By keeping some things a mystery, He keeps us dependent on Him, which is better for us in the long run, to keep us from wandering off, getting ourselves lost and in trouble.

We must accept there are some things we are simply not meant to know, so we can learn to walk by faith and not by sight.

You Can't Capture the Wind, So Adjust Your Sails

Years ago, I became interested in how the Holy Spirit works. I had pretty much neglected any thought of the third person of the Trinity save for a passing inclusion in "the Father, Son, and Holy Spirit." We know God, and we get Jesus, but the Holy Spirit is sometimes this nebulous entity that we can't quite pin down or relate to.

So I decided I would solve my unfamiliarity of the Holy Spirit through study. I carefully and painstakingly scoured the entire book of Acts and recorded the details of every encounter the earliest Christian believers had with the Holy Spirit.

After several weeks of intense study, I finally figured out the way the Holy Spirit interacts with humans. So let me help you out now by revealing what the secret formula is...there is no formula! Every encounter was tailor-made to each unique individual and circumstance.

Here's how the Holy Spirit operates: He does whatever He wants without regard to our desire for tidy rows and neatly labeled and organized containers. The Holy Spirit blows around us and through us like the wind we can neither see or control (John 3:8). All we can do is see the effects and adjust our sails.

Once again, I had to learn the hard lesson that I can't reduce God to something I can turn in my hand and scrutinize. He's just too ginormous! He's too original, too creative, and too all-encompassing to distill into a simple aphorism. He eludes compaction. We must accept Him full-size or not at all. He's not an all-powerful genie we can cram into a bottle and stuff into our pocket.

We are talking about the God who thought up the platypus after all! I believe God created the platypus for two primary reasons: to entertain Himself and to mess with human taxonomy. God will *not* be contained! And He has enough sense of humor to make a duck-billed, egg-laying, water mammal with a sixth sense to prove His point.

Divine Hide-and-Seek

It is the glory of God to conceal a matter.
It is the glory of kings to search it out.
~ Proverbs 25:2, NIV

Children consider hide-and-seek a game and a delight, not a burdensome frustration. Maybe this is part of what God means when

He encourages us to retain a child-like faith. Perhaps He wants us to delight in our mutual game of hide-and-seek without getting stressed and frustrated at the parts we can't find.

Personally, much of my angst stems from overthinking life. I like puzzles. I enjoy stretching my mind and exercising my thinker. But working on a problem, knowing the solution is and will remain out of reach, is frustrating.

The Bible doesn't come with an answer key in the back to check if we've understood and applied every verse correctly. There's no tutorial where the Instructor carefully spells out the solutions to life's most challenging questions so you can figure out exactly where your thinking went sideways.

Unsolvable Puzzles

With much wisdom comes much sorrow;
the more knowledge, the more grief.
~ Ecclesiastes 1:18, NIV

The truth is, we can't figure out the symphony of Divine Holiness with finite man anyway. This is perhaps most difficult for intellectuals or thoughtful people to accept. Their brains naturally seek to solve puzzles. Encountering quandaries that they cannot conquer is humbling in a most uncomfortable way.

We have the saying, "Ignorance is bliss," and it's true that sometimes being unaware of all you don't know makes it easier to relax and just enjoy the ride. Sometimes, intellectual thinkers have a harder time with matters of faith, but reasoning and believing are not mutually exclusive. They are meant to work together.

Knowing Does Not Bring Satisfaction

Solomon, gifted with extraordinary wisdom (1 Kings 3:12), was obviously troubled and discouraged by matters that made no sense to him, problems he couldn't figure out, and puzzles he couldn't solve. He experimented with numerous approaches to life, and in the end determined they were all "meaningless." He struggled to find the purpose of life but kept coming up short.

Solomon opens his book with, "'Meaningless! Meaningless!' says the Teacher. 'Utterly meaningless! Everything is meaningless.'" (Ecclesiastes 1:2) It's tempting to close a book and read no further when that's the opening thesis.

Solomon's pursuits "under the sun" were without the one true God at the center of everything. That's what made everything meaningless to him. It is only through a right relationship with our Maker that we find our meaning and purpose of life, for without God's eternal perspective, our brief blip of life here is meaningless outside our one moment in time.

Solomon had more wisdom and greater understanding than any person who lived before or since, yet few Biblical writers are more discouraged than he. Wisdom did not bring him satisfaction, but trusting God would have. If the wisest man who ever lived couldn't sort it all out, there's no way I'll be able to.

God has intentionally filled His Word and our world with conundrums and unsolvable puzzles. Even the most intelligent and learned scholars must admit their inability to comprehend the mysteries of God in the face of His words which are so wise they seem foolish to us at times.

The Message that points to Christ on the Cross seems like sheer silliness to those hellbent on destruction, but for those on the way of salvation it makes perfect sense. This is the way God works, and most powerfully as it turns out. It's written, "I'll turn conventional wisdom on its head, I'll expose so-called experts as crackpots." So where can you find someone truly wise, truly educated, truly intelligent in this day and age? Hasn't God exposed it all as pretentious nonsense? Since the world in all its fancy wisdom never had a clue when it came to knowing God, God in his wisdom took delight in using what the world considered dumb—preaching, of all things!—to bring those who trust him into the way of salvation. God made foolish the wisdom of this world.
~ 1 Corinthians 1:18-21, MSG

God's wisdom is so far above our abilities, it often seems foolish to the "wise" of this world. Far better to simply trust that God knows what He is doing than attempt to make Him accountable to us who possess less than a speck of the wisdom He has at His disposal.

Love, Don't Lean!

> *Trust in the Lord with all your heart and lean not on your own*
> *understanding; in all your ways submit to him, and*
> *he will make your paths straight.*
> *~ Proverbs 3:5-6, NIV*

As we just saw with Solomon, our limited understanding will never be strong enough to support our faith. We reason out what we can and trust God with the rest. It's our trust in a perfectly loving God that upholds our faith.

I believe in flying and electricity even though I don't understand them completely. I don't have a crisis of faith every time I board an airplane or flip a switch. I trust them to work according to principles I don't know intimately.

If I leaned on my understanding, I'd never get in a boat or fly in an airplane, and my house would only be lit and warmed with candles. Instead, I simply trust that the people who made these things knew what they were doing and they won't let me sink, fall or fry.

When asked what the most important thing we should do in life is, Jesus replied, "Love the Lord your God with all your heart and with all your soul and with all your mind and with all your strength." (Mark 12:30)

We are to love God with all the understanding we've got and surrender what we don't understand to Him. Don't lean on *your* understanding, trust in His. Your understanding was never meant to support the weight of life's greatest questions. Only God is strong enough to carry those. So love, don't lean!!

We Lack the Capacity

But it is the spirit in a person, the breath of the Almighty,
that gives them understanding.
~ Job 32:8, NIV

Even if we could get all the answers from God, we wouldn't comprehend them anyway.

Understanding only comes from God. We can only understand what He enables us to. Some things He prefers to keep a mystery. Some things we'd be unable to understand no matter how hard He would attempt to explain. We simply lack the capacity. It would be easier to explain nuclear fission to a dog than to explain the mysteries of God to a human.

As Shrek said to Donkey when he requested to be told he had the right to remain silent, "You have the right. It is the capacity you lack." Even if we could open and read all the books of wisdom in God's library, we would understand very little of it. We would walk away scratching our heads, still unsatisfied by the answers to our wonderings.

Oh, the depth of the riches of the wisdom and knowledge of God! How
unsearchable his judgments, and his paths beyond tracing out! "Who
has known the mind of the Lord? Or who has been his counselor?"
~ Romans 11:33-34, NIV

If we tried to download all that God knows about our lives and the universe we live in, it would literally blow up our minds. We can't handle it. God is our intellectual superior in every way. If He answered our questions in the fullness of His wisdom, we would respond with blank stares and open mouths. Our brains could not compute the meaning of His answers.

Thinking we should be able to understand everything He does only leaves us frustrated and disappointed when we can't. Instead, let's acknowledge our limited knowledge and mental capabilities, and trust what we don't understand to a God who is not only all-knowing but also all-loving.

He is the best parent that has ever existed or ever will. If He doesn't let us play ball in the street, we shouldn't get upset. We should trust that He said no because He sees the truck around the corner headed our way that we can't see yet nor comprehend the destructive force of which it is capable.

He often says no to what seems good to us because He has something far better in mind for us. What we have asked for is far too small for so great a God.

Incomprehensible Ways

Such knowledge is too wonderful for me, too lofty for me to attain.
~ Psalm 139:6, NIV

My smartphone is a great tool, but it is limited. I cannot download every app ever created. It's not that smart. There simply isn't room. Neither can my human brain hold all the wisdom and understanding that God possesses. And it's not just a matter of capacity. It's also a matter of capability.

My daughter had an older model iPhone. Recently, it tried to update itself with the latest iOS software. This futile effort from the poor outdated phone broke its mind. It was incapable of downloading information it was never designed to possess. It completely crashed, and even the good folks at the Apple store could not revive it. The data it once held was lost forever, eaten by the fried circuitry of an obsolete tool.

Don't ask God to download stuff you can't handle. Just let Him keep it safe for you, okay? If He downloaded the mysteries of the universe into your head, it would fry your circuitry.

Point of Grace has a song entitled, "Who Am I?" that says, "I stretch my mind so far I nearly come unglued." Yep, been there, done that. I've tried to stretch my mind to encompass all the wonders of God, but He refuses to be circumnavigated by mere mortals. How could a frail human brain ever comprehend the One who created it and breathed life into it?

Secret Things and Hidden Places

The LORD our God has secrets known to no one. We are not account-
able for them, but we and our children are accountable forever for all
that he has revealed to us, so that we may obey
all the terms of these instructions.
~ Deuteronomy 29:29, NLT

Wrestling too hard with the "secret" things that God has not chosen
to reveal to us only leads to frustration, disappointment, and confusion. Let's leave those to God and focus instead on what He *has*
already revealed, that we may be faithful followers even when life
doesn't make sense and His teachings are hard.

Just as you cannot understand the path of the wind or the mystery of a
tiny baby growing in its mother's womb, so you cannot understand
the activity of God, who does all things.
~ Ecclesiastes 11:5, NLT

Think of a tiny seed almost ready to sprout or an unborn child
growing hidden within her mother. There are some amazing blessings
God is growing for you in secret places. You cannot perceive them now,
but when they are ready, He will reveal them to you at the best possible time.

You may see only a patch of mud or swollen belly and think
nothing is happening and that God is not responding to your need—
but God sees what you don't. He knows all that's happening in the
secret places below the surface.

My frame was not hidden from you when
I was made in the secret place.
~ Psalm 139:15, NIV

Jesus also said, "The Kingdom of God is like a farmer who scatters
seed on the ground. Night and day, while he's asleep or awake, the
seed sprouts and grows, but he does not understand how it happens."
~ Mark 4:26-27, NLT

Every fruitful plant had to push its way through the dirt and the dark at some point. The tiny, frail immature plant had to reach for the sun it could not yet see or feel but instinctively knew was there. God puts within each plant a desire to stretch toward the life-giving radiance and warmth of the sun.

Within each seed, He stores the power and sustenance necessary to strengthen the seedling until it can poke its fragile head through the mud. If He takes such care of every grass and flower and tree, will He not meet our needs even more abundantly? We must trust that the work He does for us in secret places will be fruitful in our lives even when His ways and purposes remain hidden from us. Trust what Jesus is doing below the surface of your human perception.

As Jesus washed his disciples' feet on His last night with them, He told them, "You don't understand now what I am doing, but someday you will."(John 13:7) This is true of many perplexing things our Lord does among us. There is much we cannot fathom now, but it will not always be so. We must be patient and allow Him to unveil His masterpiece at the time of His choosing.

Look to the Cross

Since he did not spare even his own Son but gave him up for us all,
won't he also give us everything else?
~ Romans 8:32, NLT

If you fixate on your problems and unanswered questions, you will be tempted to wonder if God loves you and if He is all-powerful. But if you focus your attention on Jesus, you will know you are loved higher and longer and wider than is humanly possible, and that if Jesus can overcome death itself, there is nothing that can defeat Him. He is able, and He loves you.

We need to look no further than the cross to see that God loves us infinitely and will pay any price to rescue us from every mess.

Fringes of His Works

And these are but the outer fringe of his works; how faint the whisper
we hear of him! Who then can understand the thunder of his power?
~ Job 26:12-14, NIV

We know only a small part of what God has done. We hear only a faint whisper of all He has said. We only know a tiny fraction of all that God knows. How could we possibly set ourselves up as a judge to whether He has treated us fairly?

It is not our job to scrutinize God's Word and His activity (or perceived lack thereof) in our midst, and judge whether we think He's doing a good job or not. Who are we to tell Him whether He's right or wrong?

> Can we create a butterfly or keep the planets orbiting in their synchronized ballet of the universe? Then why do we think we are qualified to evaluate God's handiwork at all?

Can we create a butterfly or keep the planets orbiting in their synchronized ballet of the universe? Then why do we think we are qualified to evaluate God's handiwork at all?

Don't try to figure out if you think God is fair or not. Believe that He *is* fair and just. Accept that if you could know everything He knows and understand all the mysteries that He does, you would agree. It is not that God is lacking, it is that our knowledge is incomplete. That is why He often doesn't make sense to us.

God repeatedly tells us throughout the Scriptures that we ought not to even judge one another because we don't have the full story. How much less capable are we to judge The Judge Himself?

Walk by Faith, Not by Sight

"Providence looks a great way forward and has a long reach."
~ Matthew Henry

We are called to walk by faith, not by sight. We must be willing to let God be our eyes. We cannot see far enough. We are dependent upon God's infallible long-range vision and laser-precision perspective.

Believing Is Seeing

So we are always of good courage...for we walk by faith, not by sight.
~ 2 Corinthians 5:6a, 7, ESV

The world says, "Seeing is believing," but as with most things, the world's got it backwards. Jesus says believing is seeing. Check out this example from His return trip to Cana in Galilee.

In John 4:46-53, a royal officer and loving father asked Jesus for healing on behalf of his desperately ill son while Jesus was visiting Cana. This father had come from Capernaum, which was a day's uphill walk away. Consider the irony of a royal official who walked for a day to ask a poor carpenter for medical assistance. Now that's a strange 911 call.

Upon finding Jesus, the man begged Jesus to come to back to Capernaum with him. His beloved son was fatally ill, and the man believed Jesus could rescue him from death.

Instead of answering the man, Jesus turned to the crowd and accused them of having to see to believe. His statement almost seems out of place and insensitive to the desperate man pleading for his son's life.

When the man repeated his plea, Jesus told him to go home. He essentially refused the man's request to come back with him to Capernaum. But Jesus did assure him that his son would live.

Jesus didn't come to the boy in person. He didn't even say a prayer. He was just asking this man to believe in power he couldn't see and healing he couldn't understand.

I can imagine the poor man thinking, "Now what? Should I go like He says or do I stay and continue to fight for my son's life?" This was a critical faith-testing moment for this man. Much was at stake. The life of his son hung delicately in the balance.

Should he believe this man he's never met at the possible expense of his son? If I were him, I would be wondering, "What will my wife say when I return home without Jesus?"

"Believe the best about Him and you will see the best of Him."
~ Jennifer Rothschild

Now Jesus' earlier statement makes sense. He was asking him to believe without seeing. God knew he would pass this test of faith. God specifically chose this father to demonstrate that Jesus' power is unhindered by distance, and to encourage others to believe without the need to see.

Jesus pointed out to Thomas that people who believe without seeing are blessed (John 20:29). He was referring to us. Jesus doesn't sit down across the table from us to share a cup of coffee and a personal conversation. We have to believe Him without seeing Him with our physical eyes. We can't walk to Cana or anywhere else on this planet to find Jesus in the flesh.

I love verse 51, "The man took Jesus at his word and departed." Am I willing to do as much? Will I simply take Jesus at His word and stop begging Him to do something for me that I can see?

But hope that is seen is no hope at all.
Who hopes for what they already have?
~ Romans 8:24, NIV

Before the father even got back home, his servants came to meet him. They told him his son was healthy, and after a quick calculation, they determined the healing had taken place at the exact time that Jesus told him his son would live, even before the man obediently returned home as Jesus instructed.

This man came to Jesus out of personal tragedy. In desperate need and crushing grief, he acknowledged his overwhelming inadequacy to fix the situation.

Consider Hebrews, chapter 11, often referred to as the great Faith Hall of Fame. It lists people who believed God's words were true, even through hardship. They believed His promises, even in great disappointment. They persevered despite the odds stacked against them. This glorious review of heroes of the faith concludes this way.

These were all commended for their faith, yet none of them received
what had been promised, since God had planned something better...
~ *Hebrews 11:39–40a, NIV*

These people were immortalized in the Faith Hall of Fame because they chose to believe anyway. They didn't receive what they were hoping for on this earth, but they looked ahead through the eyes of faith and welcomed God's promises from a distance. Admitting they were only strangers and pilgrims passing through, they knew their real home lay in a realm beyond their physical vision.

As a result, God was "not ashamed to be called their God." (Hebrews 11:16, NIV) They lived up to the high calling of being a part of God's family. How were they able to do this? By choosing to believe anyway.

Some Things Are Better Left Unseen

One of my husband's hair-raising adventures as a fighter pilot was during a low-level mission at night through the steep mountains of Alaska. The moon was bright, but often hidden by the dense clouds. His jet is equipped with a terrain-following radar capability, which allows them to auto-fly at low altitudes at night or in the weather and at extremely fast speeds.

It's nerve-wracking for a fighter pilot to let the jet do the flying, especially 500 feet above the ground in the mountains at over 500 mph, all while in the clouds or dark of night. One must be able to trust their aircraft systems over their desire to take control.

At one point in Joel's flight, there was a clear patch of sky with no clouds and the moon's light reflected brightly off the snow-covered mountains. As my husband looked at the ragged mountains towering jaggedly high above him on either side, he suddenly became more appreciative of the proximity of the threat.

He had known they were there, but laying eyes on the mountain range revealed the true magnitude of the hazard. God only shows us what we need to see. Sometimes, He hides our path from us because if we see it, we might be too afraid to follow Him there.

Somebody's Missing

After our second child was born, I wondered if our family was complete. We had two children, a boy and a girl. We were "just right," according to our cultural norms. I prayed and asked God if this was how He wanted our family to be. An undeniable certainty rose within me. I knew that if we stopped growing our family then, I would always feel like someone was missing.

At the time, of course, I had no idea *how many* somebodies were missing! If God had told me then that I would go on to have six more children and a bonus son in Heaven, and that He would call me to homeschool them, I confess I would have been very tempted to run the other direction!

Fortunately, He was wise enough to only reveal to me as much as I needed to know to take the next step. I wasn't ready for Him to unveil the entire family plan just yet. I had some growing to do before I could consider, much less agree, to go along with the mission He had in mind.

A Flashlight, Not a Spotlight

Think of a time you didn't know about a danger or problem until after the fact. Have you ever said, "I'm glad I didn't know"? Knowing everything that lies ahead won't make you more peaceful. In fact, it might make your anxiety worse when you catch a glimpse of the jagged rocks God is steering you through.

God is wise enough to know what you need to see and what you don't. He won't withhold anything you need to know to take the next step on the path He has for you. Nor will He disclose anything that you don't need to know that may throw you off course. Sometimes He keeps things hidden for your own good.

The Psalmist tells us that God's word is like a flashlight we shine on our path at night, so we don't trip (Psalms 119:105). God gives us a flashlight, not necessarily a spotlight. He doesn't usually enter the room and flip the light switch revealing everything at once. We would be overwhelmed! He shows us what's just ahead and tells us to follow Him, putting our feet in His footprints so we can stay firmly on the right path.

A God of the Clouds

I find it interesting that in Scripture, God often visits His people in clouds. God led Moses and the Israelites out of slavery and to the Promised Land from a pillar of cloud (Exodus 13:21). Matthew. Sinai was shrouded in dark clouds as God spoke to Moses and gave them the Law (Exodus 19:16). Clouds filled the tabernacle (Exodus 40:34), and later, the temple when the presence of the Lord descended upon them (2 Chronicles 5:14).

Clouds surrounded Jesus, Peter, James, and John at His transfiguration (Luke 9:34). Jesus returned to Heaven following His resurrection with an escort of clouds (Acts 1:9), and clouds will accompany Him when He returns to Earth (Mark 13:26, Revelation 1:7). We will join Him in the clouds as we are resurrected in glory (1 Thessalonians 4:17).

God often chooses to come to us shrouded in mystery. He remains hidden from complete disclosure until the proper time, and we must remain assured that this too is for our benefit.

No Image of God

Almost all ancient religions had statues of their gods with one major exception—the Israelites. In fact, they were the opposite. God instructed them in His second commandment not to make any image for the purpose of worship (Exodus 20:4-5). Why would He say that?

We *want* to *see* God. We think it will make our faith easier. Even Jesus' disciples who had one person of the Trinity at the table with them requested to see God. "Just show us the Father, and that will be enough." Will it?

God was already sitting right in front of them, and they weren't getting it! Even Jesus seems slightly exasperated with them at this point. "Don't you know me after I've been with you so long?" He seems pained that they still do not recognize Him as God (John 14: 8-9).

Because we cannot see God with our physical eyes, it is very tempting to imagine Him as we'd like Him to be rather than how He is. Do you notice the root-word "image" in "imagine"?

Now we may not have any statues that we bow down and worship, so we may claim that idolatry is not much of a temptation for us. But how many times have we tried to make God in our own image when the truth He presents is hard to swallow?

Imagine means to create a mental image of something using our intellect rather than our physical senses. That's what we do when we picture God to be someone other than who He has revealed Himself to be through His Word. Jesus came, in part, to show us what God looks like. Any God image we create that is inconsistent with who Jesus actually is becomes idolatry.

Face to Face with God

I believe God put this desire to see Him face to face within us because that is what He plans to bring about when all is said and done. Now, we see only a fuzzy reflection of God as though we are looking at Him via a warped and scratched mirror. But one day, we *will* see Him face to face (1 Corinthians 13:12).

> *Now we see things imperfectly, like puzzling reflections in a mirror, but then we will see everything with perfect clarity. All that I know now is partial and incomplete, but then I will know everything completely, just as God now knows me completely.*
> *~ 1 Corinthians 13:12, NLT*

Right now, we know only in part. It's fuzzy and dim, but hold on. Trust Jesus, who gave up everything for you, and wait patiently for the day when you see Him face to face. Then all your confusion will melt away, and all your questions will dissolve in perfect clarity. God will wipe every tear from your eyes, and His love will shine so bright that we will no longer have any need of the sun, much less our trusty old flashlight that lit the way of our pilgrimage.

> *"He will afterwards reconcile us to all the dark providences that now puzzle and perplex us."*
> *~ Matthew Henry*

Once we arrive in Eternity, our understanding will mushroom exponentially. I wonder, will God still reserve a few mysteries only for Himself? Will He retain some mystery even when we are with Him in Eternity?

Perhaps not everything we question now will be made known someday. One day, our questions will either all be answered, or they will simply cease to matter to us and be forgotten in light of Eternity.

We can't even begin to imagine how wonderful that will be. All questions answered, all puzzles solved, all wrongs made right. And every believer will be standing healed and whole, with all tears wiped dry—face to face with the Living God.

We will be able to do what the Israelites (Deuteronomy 5:25-26) and Daniel (Daniel 10:8) and John (Revelation 1:17) could not— stand face to face with Jesus in all His majesty and look Him in the eye without shame.

That. Is. Mind blowing.

Acknowledge Both Doubt and Faith

Until the day we see Jesus face to face, we must learn to embrace the tension of feeling both doubt and faith at the same time. Like the people who interacted with Jesus in person, we are all a mixture of faith and doubt of varying proportions.

It is best to acknowledge rather than attempt to deny the tension these two opposing forces exert on our hearts and minds. We must also be willing to give each other grace and safe places to voice both our doubts and our faith.

This is necessary to move into deeper levels of understanding. Stuffing doubts only keeps us stuck. Whereas, crying truthfully out, "I do believe, help me overcome my unbelief!" marks an important step toward choosing to believe anyway, even when God doesn't make sense.

Where Else Can I Go?

One day, Jesus fed 5,000-plus people with one boy's lunch. That night, He walked across the stormy Sea of Galilee to comfort His disciples and calm the storm that raged around them.

The next morning, the crowd found Jesus on the other side of the lake after searching for Him and wondering where He had gone. Jesus called them out on their motives and revealed that it was their bellies rather than their spiritual hunger that led them to search for Him.

He then declared Himself to be the Bread of Life who would completely satisfy all their hunger. They didn't get His metaphor. They grumbled and scoffed. But then it got worse. Check out this doozy Jesus dropped on them.

> *"I tell you the truth, unless you eat the flesh of the Son of Man and drink his blood, you cannot have eternal life within you. But anyone who eats my flesh and drinks my blood has eternal life, and I will raise that person at the last day. For my flesh is true food, and my blood is true drink."*
> *~ John 6:53b-55, NLT*

Yowza! They weren't ready for that! We can handle it because we're reading His statement from this side of the resurrection. We practice communion and are therefore accustomed to pairing Jesus' body and blood with eating and drinking.

The people listening to Jesus that day didn't have such advantages to aid their understanding, and Jesus didn't seem to explain Himself either. Try to imagine this teaching from their perspective!

No wonder many of His followers decided they had heard enough and left, never to return (John 6:66). I can't say I blame them. If a traveling preacher came to my church and started speaking about the benefits of cannibalism in relation to my spiritual life, I think I'd leave too.

At this point, Jesus turned to the Twelve and asked them if they were also offended (John 6:61b). Their response was not recorded in Scripture. I wish it were! He asked them, *"Do you want to leave me too?"* (John 6:67).

Of course, we can count on bold Peter to speak up.

> *"Lord, to whom shall we go? You have the words of eternal life. We have come to believe and to know that you are the Holy One of God."*
> *~ John 6:68-69, NIV*

Peter's response is reminiscent of Asaph's words, "Whom have I in heaven but you? And earth has nothing I desire besides you." (Psalm 73:25)

In my dark night of wandering in faithless valleys and meandering through the doubting corners of my mind, I allowed myself to consider other options for the first time in my life. If I couldn't count on God to be all that He claimed to be, then what *did* I believe?

I got dangerously close to walking away with the crowd that was confused and conflicted by Jesus' command to eat His flesh. God was starting to sound about that crazy to me, and I thought it was time to consider more rational alternatives.

I didn't dig very far into any other religions or worldviews, because I already knew enough to know why they didn't solve humanity's most pressing problems or satisfy our greatest needs. As I wandered and wondered, Peter's refrain followed me expectantly like a devoted puppy, always at my heels wagging its tail. "Where else can I go, Jesus? You alone are able to lead me to my true life and destiny."

I was stuck. There I lay, wounded and bleeding from daring to live life God's way with nowhere else to go. I knew in my head and my heart that there was no way to freedom and victory without Jesus. So I turned around and came back.

I let the offended masses walk past me in disgust, and pressed forward to stand with Peter and Asaph and many others next to Jesus. With them, my heart cried out, "I don't get it, God! It sounds weird and disgusting and even wrong. But you're God, and I have nowhere else to go. There is no one else to rescue me, no other name by which I can be saved. If I don't find eternal life in You, I'm not getting it anywhere else. Where else can I go? Whom have I in Heaven but You?"

I learned by their example that it's okay to be confused but still committed nonetheless. The disciples and the psalmist recognized that God might be hard to understand, but there's no one else to turn to who has all the answers. We must learn to accept, embrace, and lean into the mystery to behold God as He is, not as we'd wish Him to be.

It can be very tempting to walk away from Jesus when life is too hard, difficult to understand, or when it just hurts too much. Before you walk away, ask yourself, "Where else can I go?" Are your other options any better? He alone offers you eternal life. Why don't you stick around and choose to believe anyway? You have nothing to lose and Eternity to gain.

Time to Get Off the Fence

"How long will you waver between two opinions?
If the LORD is God, follow him..."
~ 1 Kings 18:21, NIV

Don't try to hold it back until you have all the answers. You'll never have all the answers this side of Heaven. You weren't meant to. Quit striving and squirming in the midst of your lack of answers to big questions. Rest in the mysteries of His love and wisdom, and choose to believe anyway, even when it seems like you shouldn't.

Now that we've dealt with our questions and doubts, we are ready to engage the battle that surrounds us, ready to stand strong in our faith. But before we can experience victory, we must know the nature of the conflict that engulfs us and who the players are. In the next chapter, we will talk about the battle we face and the enemy that hunts us.

PART II

UNBEATABLE: THE ROAD
OF TRIUMPH

Life is a battlefield, not a playground.
Knowing your enemy, your God, and yourself enables
you to live victoriously.

*For we are not fighting against flesh-and-blood enemies, but against
evil rulers and authorities of the unseen world, against mighty powers
in this dark world, and against evil spirits in the heavenly places.*

Ephesians 6:12, NLT

If you don't know the plans of your enemy, the power of your God, and your own true identity, you will never experience lasting victory in this life. If you don't understand the nature of the fight, you will lose every time.

Resist your enemy. Trust your God and surrender to Him. Be confident in who God says you are.

It's called the road of triumph, not the place of triumph, because life is a journey, not a destination. You will never "arrive" at a permanent place of victory this side of Heaven. There is no place in life where you can say, "I've made it. Now I can coast." Life is a battle to the end.

Your permanent victory lies on the other side. You must pass through Death to get there, but Death can't keep you because Jesus broke the power of the Grave over you. You can live free and undefeated, even as you engage in the battle that rages around you.

CHAPTER 5

THE BATTLE: KNOW YOUR ENEMY

Revealing Your Ultimate Battle

"If you know the enemy and know yourself, you need not fear the result of a hundred battles. If you know yourself but not the enemy, for every victory gained you will also suffer a defeat. If you know neither the enemy nor yourself, you will succumb in every battle."
~ *Sun Tzu*, The Art of War

Not Your Enemy

God is not your enemy. People are not your enemy. Circumstances are not your enemy. You are not even your own enemy (though you sometimes cooperate with him). You have an enemy, but it's none of these.

Truth Detection Officer

After graduating from the Academy, I served on active duty in the Air Force for several years before switching careers to motherhood. One of my more interesting job titles was the Wing Tactical Deception Officer.

It was my job to help the operational squadrons practice deceiving our enemies. I was trained in ways to make military forces appear different than they were with the sole purpose of causing the enemy to respond in inappropriate and ineffective ways.

This is an excellent metaphor for what our enemy tries to do to us. For too long, I have responded to life in inappropriate and ineffective ways because I failed to understand the nature of the struggle I was in and the schemes of my enemy.

If I could pick a new duty title now, it would be Truth Detection Officer. Let's expose the truth about the war we fight and the enemy who deceives us, so we can stop fighting the wrong battles.

Acknowledge the War

How effective would the armed forces of our country be if they failed to acknowledge the battle in which they were engaged? How many would be taken out or taken captive by the enemy if they had no idea who the enemy was?

Many of us do not recognize the truth that we live our lives in a war zone. We think life is meant to be an amusement park. It is so easy for us to become distracted by pleasure seeking and fail to realize we are in a fight for our lives. It is common to be so busy struggling with other people that we misidentify our real enemy.

How often do we miss the fact that our primary battle is spiritual? Yet, if we are not standing strong spiritually, we aren't standing up at all.

If you do not stand firm in your faith, you will not stand at all.
~ Isaiah 7:9b, NIV

If we're going to live victoriously, we must learn to identify our real fight. The essential first step to living an undefeated life is to acknowledge the cosmic battle of good versus evil raging around us at all times. To deny that truth is to be already defeated. Instead, we are called to be ready, be alert, and to resist him.

Battle Ready

A Christian life does not equal a carefree life. Don't be surprised by trouble or be caught off guard. God never promised us easy lives—quite the opposite, in fact. Many Scriptures warn us of the inevitability of troubles and pain.

*Consider it pure joy, my brothers and sisters, whenever you face trials
of many kinds, because you know that the testing
of your faith produces perseverance.*
~ James 1:2-3, NIV

James says, "Whenever you face trials of many kinds..." (James 1:2) Not "if," but "when." You *will* face trials. We don't have a choice about that. Our only choice is how we respond to those trials.

For some reason, many Christians think that life with Jesus is supposed to be all sunshine and roses. I used to be a victim of that false belief. I would grab hold of the promised victory and answered prayer, somehow missing the thorns among the roses.

We know roses have thorns and so we handle them accordingly. Friends, I hate to break it to you, but the Christian life has some pretty nasty thorns too (Psalms 34:19, 2 Timothy 3:12, 1 Peter 4:12). The thorns in no way detract from the beauty of the roses, but we must still acknowledge they are there and deal with life appropriately, and with a proper mindset.

Jesus Himself is our perfect example. He walked on water, healed the sick, and gave sight to the blind, but He was also falsely accused, mercilessly tortured, and faithlessly abandoned. Before He could experience glorious and miraculous resurrection, He had to experience a cruel and humiliating death. If perfect Jesus suffered so greatly, how can we expect to sail through life unscathed and unscarred?

Satan's schemes and attacks are just a fact of life, and being a follower of Christ doesn't mean you are exempt. Recognize you are in a battle and therefore you will be attacked, *especially* if you are trying to love and serve God.

Brace Yourself

Imagine for a moment that you knew someone was about to try and knock you over, and you needed to brace yourself to keep standing. What would you do physically?

You would secure a firm footing and lean into the forces coming against you. You would automatically tighten your muscles to resist hard and push back if you knew a shove was coming. If you get caught off guard without an opportunity to brace yourself, you will be sure to fall hard.

Now take that same mental picture you just created and do that spiritually. Be aware of possible attacks and brace yourself to withstand them. Secure your footing on the firm foundation of Jesus' words (Matthew 7:24-25). Resist your enemy and push back. Resolve to stand strong as long as you can, and get back up by the power of God's grace when you fall.

We must accept ahead of time that we will have trouble and be ready to lean hard on God when it comes. When we are ready to face trials, they will lose the power of a surprise attack. We won't get caught off guard, but we will be able to stand strong in the power of Christ.

Hope for the Battle Ahead

Not only must we expect trials, let's not forget to expect God to be present with us and provide for us in the midst of adversity. The enemy will launch all kinds of junk at us, but we can move forward with peace and joy knowing our God is greater than anything that our enemy can launch against us (1 John 4:4, Isaiah 54:17).

This attitude of readiness can easily become an Eeyore mentality if we do not keep it in check. God calls us to be vigilant, not paranoid. Expecting disaster to befall at any moment and looking for certain danger around every corner will not help us to live the joyful life of abundance that Jesus wants us to have.

Always balance your preparation for battle with a healthy dose of living fully in and enjoying the moment God has given right now. God has plans and preparations for a hopeful future for us (Jeremiah 29:11). Don't forget that part either! Yes, struggles are headed your way, but God's already planned for that, and He's already got it covered. Lean on Him!

I have told you these things, so that in me you may have peace.
In this world you will have trouble. But take heart!
I have overcome the world.
~ John 16:33, NIV

Acknowledge Your Enemy

It is imperative that you know who your enemy is. If you misidentify your enemy or deny that you have one, you will lose the battle before it begins. The first step to knowing your enemy is to acknowledge that there *is* an enemy.

How successful would a soldier be if she refused to believe the enemy she fought was real? If someone broke into your home or threatened you on the street, you wouldn't ignore *that* enemy and just hope they'd go away, would you?

Yet, that's what so many of us do when it comes to our spiritual battles. Your real enemy is far more dangerous than the threats you can see.

God instructs us to resist the devil. We must acknowledge something to resist it. Refusing to acknowledge the presence and threat of your enemy is disastrous in any battle.

The Devil is Not a Myth

Many people, Christians even, think of Satan as a cartoon, legend, fable, fairytale, or a metaphor. There is great danger in believing our enemy is a fictitious fairytale character. It is very difficult, if not impossible, to live victoriously with this view. Getting beat up by an enemy you can't see and won't acknowledge is extremely defeating.

Satan will try to convince us he doesn't exist at all, enabling him to operate in ultimate stealth mode. If we think there is no threat, we will let our guard down, making ourselves easier targets.

Often, not only are we failing to watch out for our enemy but when trouble does come, we tend to blame God instead of the actual perpetrator. That's a double win for the devil and a huge defeat for us.

The fact that we can't see him doesn't make him any less real than God. He is better able to successfully ambush us if we aren't even aware that he exists, leaving us wondering, "How did *this* happen? Where did *that* come from?"

The devil is not a harmless myth. He is a dangerously vicious enemy. How can anyone look at all that goes on in this world and not believe in a source and prompter of evil?

If the devil were merely a myth or a metaphor, then we are hard-pressed to explain why Jesus Himself urged us to pray daily for deliverance against the evil one (Matthew 6:13). If Jesus took Satan seriously, then so must we.

Threat Misidentification

Before Japan's attack on Pearl Harbor in 1941, military leadership attempted to thwart a presumed threat of local Japanese-Americans. At Hickman Field, they decided to pull the Army Air Corps planes out of the hangars, bunch them together on the open runway, and unload all weapons, thinking this would protect them from any local hostiles trying to sneak into the hangars to sabotage the aircraft.

In actuality, they had lined them up as easy targets for the real enemy who soared overhead and bombed them from the skies. The American forces were completely caught off guard by this surprise attack from an enemy they did not expect.

They grossly underestimated the reach of their adversary and did not take necessary precautions from the real threat. It was their very efforts at security that left them most vulnerable to attack.

The cost of this miscalculation was catastrophic. Only five U.S. aircrafts were able to get airborne and fight back against the Japanese. The destruction of American aircraft, naval ships, and loss of life dealt a devastating blow.

Because American leadership misidentified their enemy, they prepared for the wrong fight and were nearly disabled during the battle. We often make similar miscalculations in our lives and the results are just as destructive.

If you are feeling defeated, is it possible you are fighting the wrong fight or engaging the wrong enemy? Maybe you've experienced a crushing setback because you have been blindsided by your real enemy while you were focused on someone or something that was not actually a true threat.

A tactic Satan often employs is to attempt to confuse us about who our enemy is. He wants to make us think our enemy is someone else. While we're preoccupied fighting the wrong battles against a person or situation who is not our real enemy, we allow him to slip into our lives "below the radar" undetected and unchallenged.

Fight the Right Fight

When Joshua and the Israelites went to fight the city of Ai, they concentrated solely on the physical battle. Fresh off an astounding underdog upset at Jericho, they completely forgot how they'd won the previous battle. They spied out what they were up against and decided they only needed a couple of thousand soldiers to defeat this smaller enemy.

They were utterly crushed. The men of Ai drove them out of the city and killed several of them as they fled. The Israelites were terror-stricken. Their courage melted like ice cream on a hot day. They scampered home soundly defeated with their tails between their legs.

Joshua then did what he should have done first. He went to God and sought His direction. God explained the reason for their defeat was because of their flagrant disobedience after the last battle. Against God's explicit orders, one man, Achan, had stolen some spoils of war for himself, lied about it, and hidden them in his tent.

> There's no such thing as victorious disobedience. It doesn't exist. If you want to win, you have to play by God's rules.

Listen, folks. God knows what's buried under your tent. You can't hide from Him, so don't bother trying. You can't win and do your own thing at the same time. There's no such thing as victorious disobedience. It doesn't exist. If you want to win, you have to play by God's rules.

Achan learned this the hard way. He traded his victory for gold, silver, and a pretty robe. And his disobedience didn't just hurt himself. He brought defeat and death to his family, his fellow soldiers, and the whole young nation of Israel—over a few earthly treasures that wouldn't last anyway.

Joshua and his men lost the battle because they were fighting the wrong fight. They thought their fight was with Ai (and eventually it was), but that day, their true battle was against disobedience and disrespect of God. The real fight was with greed, deceit, and betrayal. Those were the enemies that kicked their tails that day.

Fight the Good Fight

Like the Israelites on that fateful day, our most significant conflict is fought along spiritual fronts. The physical wars we get caught waging in are usually just distractions.

Satan's goal is to distract us from the prize by keeping us engaged in the wrong fight. If we don't fight the right fight, we'll lose every time. Our enemy knows that. Do we?

Fight the good fight for the true faith. Hold tightly to the eternal life to which God has called you, which you have confessed so well before many witnesses.
~ 1 Timothy 6:12, NLT

The good fight is the right fight. We must choose our battles wisely and fight for that which is of eternal consequence. Let's not waste our energy and get distracted by petty squabbles that have no significance beyond today. We need to fight hard against evil by fighting *for* the people who are getting beaten or are in bondage.

Friend or Foe?

The ability to accurately identify friend from foe is paramount to the successful outcome of any battle. Attacking the wrong target has devastating and irreversible consequences.

As a first-year cadet at the Academy, the upperclassmen frequently quizzed us on the identity of various aircraft silhouettes throughout our freshman year. We were expected to be able to tell an American F-16 from a Soviet MiG-21 with only a quick glance at the outline of the aircraft.

During one particular training weekend, the upperclassmen took delight in making the exercise more difficult by simulating the chaos of a real-world aerial dogfight. We were taken one at a time to a dark room and seated in a rolling desk chair facing a projection on the wall. One upperclassman flashed various silhouettes in rapid-fire and demanded we yell "friend" or "foe" according to which country the aircraft belonged.

All the while, two additional upperclassmen grabbed each side of the chair and shook it as violently as possible without tossing us across the room. A fourth upperclassman sprayed water in our faces and verbally assaulted us as a nuisance and to further disrupt our vision. I'm unconvinced of the effectiveness of this particular training method or the realism of it, but the upperclassmen sure enjoyed it.

The point is, if your country is going to trust you with lethal weapons and send you out to fight for freedom's cause, you better be able to distinguish who to trust from who to fire upon.

As soldiers of the cross in the Lord's army, we too must be certain of who exactly we are called to fight against and who we are called to protect.

Wrestle Not

If I asked you, "Who is your enemy?", what would you say? You may be thinking of a particular person or a certain situation, like an illness, financial hardship, or misfortune.

But while certain people and situations can be difficult and painful, none of those are our true enemies. Though we face many trials, they are not our enemy. The people and circumstances that batter us are not where we should be fighting.

> *Put on all of God's armor so that you will be able to stand firm*
> *against all strategies of the devil. For we are not fighting against*
> *flesh-and-blood enemies, but against evil rulers and authorities of the*
> *unseen world, against mighty powers in this dark world,*
> *and against evil spirits in the heavenly places.*
> *~ Ephesians 6:11-12, NLT*

Ephesians 6:12 tells us that the people in our lives are not the real problem. The powers of darkness that entangle both them and us are our true enemies. It's not any person in your life or situation facing you that is tripping you up and causing your struggle. It is the very devil himself who prowls around looking for someone to chew up and spit out.

Our adversary wants us to think our enemies are the people and situations around us. If we become distracted, wrestling with each other and life circumstances, we won't wrestle against our real foe.

While our guns are aimed in the wrong direction, he is able to steal our victory out from under us. We are warriors, but we must be careful not to misidentify our enemy. The Bible is clear on how our struggle is never against people, but against the powers of evil that threaten to undo us all.

Break the Teeth of the Wicked?

I used to struggle with the more violent prayers in the Psalms, mostly of David calling down various curses upon his enemies. This didn't sound like the prayer of a man after God's own heart to me!

The fancy description for prayers invoking God's judgment and wrath upon his enemies is "imprecatory." Imprecate means to pray evil against or invoke curses upon another—like when David asks God to bust up his enemies' faces.

Arise, Lord! Deliver me, my God! Strike all my enemies on the jaw;
break the teeth of the wicked.
~ Psalm 3:7, NIV

Really? Was I supposed to pray *that* about people who were giving me trouble? I didn't think so. I mean, it's one thing to ask to be delivered from the oppression of your enemies, but smashing their faces is something else. I don't think this is quite what Jesus had in mind when He told us to pray for our enemies.

Redefining My Enemy

My whole perspective shifted many years ago when I read *Hind's Feet on High Places.* The way Hannah Hurnard personified the bad guys in her allegory enlightened me.

The story is about a woman named Much-Afraid and her journey with the Chief Shepherd to the Kingdom of Love. She flees the Valley of Humiliation where she lives when she is forced to marry Craven Fear who intimidates her.

In fact, the whole Fearing Family is against her. Her cousin, Coward, tries to choke her and discourage her from traveling with the Chief Shepherd. Gloomy guards her until she risks calling out for Mrs. Valiant to free her.

Sorrow and Suffering are her companions throughout her difficult journey, sent by the Chief Shepherd to teach her things she could not learn otherwise. Ultimately, Much Afraid overcomes her enemies by her love of the Chief Shepherd and His love for her.

This book opened my eyes to who my enemies *really* are. Now I read the violent Psalms as a metaphor for what I ask of God regarding my spiritual enemies.

My enemies are not people. My enemies are fear, sin, deceit, lies, unbelief, cowardice and the like, which all originate from our only real enemy—Satan. And I have no problem at all asking God to break *his* "teeth" and thwart his devouring bite.

I Have an Enemy, and It's Not You!

When I feel that I am in conflict with another person, I remind myself, "I have an enemy, and it's not you." I don't say this out loud, of course! I don't want to freak the other person out. But it does help me to re-cage my focus to where the real battle lies and not get caught up in the diversion.

Even the kindest and most upright people on the planet are flawed. Everyone makes selfish decisions or foolish mistakes from time to time. But although you may have an argument, disagreement, or even a full-out fight with your family member or friend, he or she is *not* your enemy. You are both on the same team whether you acknowledge it or not.

Your real enemy is the spirit of pride, sin, deceit, or addiction that lies behind your loved one's hurtful words and actions (as well as your own).

As long as we continue to fight against and resist other people, we are not fighting back or resisting the devil, and we are playing right into his hands. He'd love to keep us so busy arguing with each other that we don't have the time, effort, or energy to oppose him.

Think back over the past week. Can you identify any conflicts where your passion and energy were wasted fighting with a fellow soldier instead of joining forces with him to turn against your common foe?

Warriors & Neighbors

Jesus replied, "You must love the LORD your God with all your heart, all your soul, and all your mind.' This is the first and greatest commandment. A second is equally important: 'Love your neighbor as yourself.' The entire law and all the demands of the prophets are based on these two commandments."
~ Matthew 22:37-40, NLT

People entrapped in the devil's deceptions are like POWs captured by the enemy. We fight, not against them but for them, because we have all fallen prey to those pretty lies at one time or another. God calls us to resist the devil—not each other.

The people in our lives, no matter how challenging they may be at times, are on our side. They may be wounded or captured by the enemy forces. The enemy may have indoctrinated them with his sweet-sounding lies, but we must never give them up for lost.

God calls us to rescue and free, to bind up and heal—not to batter the wounded or snub the POWs. Rather than allowing the defeated ones to pull us down, let us lift them up and show them where true victory lives.

God calls us to love our neighbors and resist our enemy. We must do both.

All people are our neighbors, never our enemies. It is against the schemes of Satan that we must fight. And fight hard!

We must always love the people harassed by these relentless enemies, no matter how broken or beat up we find them. Jesus calls us to be the Good Samaritan who offers healing and hope instead of just passing by or avoiding uncomfortable encounters.

Love always protects and defends. A mother's love for her child is both tender toward the child and fierce toward anything that threatens her child. True love is not for the wimpy or faint of heart.

- Jesus-love means we step out and stand up, saying, "Not on my watch!" to the evil forces that threaten to engulf us.

- Jesus-love means we reach out to the lonely, forgotten, ignored, outcast, defeated, and broken.

- Jesus-love means we are absolutely a kind and generous neighbor to every person that crosses our path.

But we never cozy up with bigotry, judgment, or injustice—these are not meant to be our neighbors. These attitudes and their associates must be kicked to the curb and never welcomed in our midst.

Embrace all people like a good neighbor. Resist all evil like a mighty warrior. Live boldly, love extravagantly, and fight courageously. Just be sure you're fighting the right battle and not attacking the ones you are called to defend.

Can you think of anyone within your range who may have felt the sting of "friendly fire" from your misguided "missiles"? Re-identify your target. It's not your neighbor, or your spouse, or your boss. Re-engage in the right fight with your true enemies and the sin that crouches at the door to your heart ready to snatch you (Genesis 4:7).

> Just be sure you're fighting the right battle and not attacking the ones you are called to defend.

Know Your Enemy

Once you admit your life is a battle, acknowledge you have an enemy, and successfully identify who your enemy is, the next step is to gather some intel on the nature of your enemy so you are equipped for the final step—resisting him. So let's do a little reconnaissance mission and spy on the enemy camp to see what we can learn.

Satan's Backstory: The Making of an Enemy

There are a few key passages that tell us the story of our enemy: Ezekiel 28:12-19; Isaiah 14:12-17; Revelation 12:7-13, 17; and Revelation 20:1-3, 7-10. From these Scriptures, we learn who Satan was created to be, who he chose to become instead, who he is now, and what will become of him in the end.

The Shining One

"You were the model of perfection, full of wisdom
and exquisite in beauty."
~ Ezekiel 28:12b, NLT

Originally, God created a beautiful, powerful, and intelligent angelic being called Heylel, in Hebrew. We usually use the more common name, Lucifer, which is Latin based. His name communicated the idea of shining brightness, and he was a specimen of radiant perfection, adorned with sparkling jewels.

God appointed him as a guardian, and he dwelt in the presence of God. He was a blameless and wise ruler who shone like the sun in bright purity. Lucifer held a high position of honor and authority, but he wanted more.

The Pride of Not Enough

For you said to yourself, "I will ascend to heaven and set my throne
above God's stars. I will preside on the mountain of the gods
far away in the north. I will climb to the highest heavens
and be like the Most High."
~ Isaiah 14:13-14, NLT

Being second in command over all Creation was not enough to satisfy Lucifer's pride and envy. He felt he was superior to the rest of God's creation and even to God himself. His exquisite beauty and unmatched intelligence inflated his vulnerable ego with pride. Interestingly, the same Hebrew word Heylel, which means "shining one," can also reference pride or self-glory.

Lucifer decided that being gifted and honored **by God** was not enough. He wanted to **be God**.

The Arrogance of Rebellion

His misguided ambition led him to orchestrate a rebellion against God to usurp the throne. Perhaps through some sly deception, he persuaded a third of God's angel army to join him.

Each one of God's angels made a permanent and unchangeable decision regarding who to serve, the Rightful Ruler or the illegitimate insurgent. Two-thirds remained loyal to the rightful King of Creation, but the other third joined the rebellion.

Since God's righteous justice cannot tolerate such an arrogant insurrection, God was forced to expel the devil and his followers from Heavenly realms and cast them down to earth.

> *Then war broke out in heaven. Michael and his angels fought against the dragon, and the dragon and his angels fought back. But he was not strong enough, and they lost their place in heaven. The great dragon was hurled down—that ancient serpent called the devil, or Satan, who leads the whole world astray. He was hurled to the earth, and his angels with him.*
> *~ Revelation 12:7-9, NIV*

The Humiliation of Rejection

Whatever he hoped to achieve was denied. God was still on His throne, but the prideful cherub was now even worse off than before. In the bitterness of defeat, he fled the court of the King of Kings and was flung to a lower realm, far from the beauty and glory of Heaven, but still under the authority and power of the Almighty.

Driven from the presence of God in shameful disgrace, Satan became a spectacle of humiliation to all creation and a warning to any who refuse to stay humble before the Lord. He who was once exalted and admired became loathed and rejected, thrown out like unwanted trash.

He was disfigured and openly humiliated as the universe looked on. Once so gloriously beautiful, he strayed into vanity and self-worship; the "shining one" was consumed by his own internal fire and looked upon with disdain and disgust (Ezekiel 28:18-19).

Created Good, Chose Evil

God did not create Satan as evil. God created Lucifer as good, beautiful, and wise, and He bestowed him with the gift of freedom. God is good, and freedom is good. However, when freedom is used to make choices that are contrary to God's best plan, evil results.

It was Lucifer's own rebellious choice to become the devil. He transformed himself into evil, twisted himself from an angel of light to an agent of darkness, corrupting all that God had created for good into wickedness, envy, and murder.

This tragic fall from a high and honored position to a dark abyss of disgrace was neither God's intention nor His doing. Lucifer's prideful rebellion brought it upon himself.

Misery Loves Company

Having chosen to reject all God had given him because he craved even more, he now attempts to entice us to follow his lead. Appallingly, he allowed the gifts of his surpassing beauty and intellect to inflate his view of himself, and he tries to persuade us to do likewise.

Considering himself superior even to God, he rejected his rightful place of humble submission under the authority of his Creator. He forgot that he owed all he was to God and desired more than he already had. How often do we humans fall into this same pit of greed?

Rather than being grateful for his blessings, he coveted the one thing he could not have. If you'll recall, this is the same sin he tempted Adam and Eve to commit—to desire the *one thing* that was off limits. Frequently, it is the same strategy he uses to seduce us to join his rebellion against Our Adonai unknowingly.

A New Name

A change in character requires a change in name. Thus Lucifer, the Shining One, became Satan, the Adversary or Accuser. His Greek name, the devil, means divider, separator or slanderer.

Jesus referred to him as "the evil one" (Matthew 13:19), "the father of lies" (John 8:44), and "the prince of this world" (John

12:31; 14:30; 16:11), while the Pharisees called him "Beelzebul, the prince of demons" (Matthew 12:24).

Later, Paul called him "the god of this age" (2 Corinthians 4:4) and "the prince of the power of the air" (Ephesians 2:2). In the final book of the Bible, God identifies him as the "deceiver of the whole world" (Revelation 12:9).

Disarmed by Christ

And having disarmed the powers and authorities, he made a public spectacle of them, triumphing over them by the cross.
~ Colossians 2:15, NIV

Jesus triumphed over Satan and all evil powers by sacrificing Himself and defeating death to rise again (Hebrews 2:14). He publicly defamed the forces of darkness in spiritual realms. The devil knows this, but he doesn't want you and me to know it. His desire is to keep up the ruse that we are the defeated ones, for as long as he can.

Defeated, But Dangerous

Even though the devil is defeated, he is still dangerous. Imagine a mighty dragon struck with a fatal blow, thrashing wildly in the throes of death. He is conquered and restricted, but can still swipe at us with his massive tail or piercing claws.

The time has not yet come for us to let down our defenses entirely. John tells us the whole world lies in the power of the evil one (1 John 5:19).

Like a rogue underling left in charge while the Master is away, he uses his powers for evil, not good. He always opposes, rather than cooperate with God's perfect will. He is still in defiant rebellion against the true Ruler of this realm, even though he knows his cause is hopeless.

His power and influence are limited to what God ultimately uses for His good and noble purposes. God does not allow Satan free-reign. Everything He allows the devil to do, He has plans to redeem. We humans don't always cooperate with God's redeeming plans, but they exist, nonetheless.

The power of evil in this world never exceeds or even equals the power of God. He always has been and always will be subject to God whether he admits it or not.

Destruction of Evil

The conclusion of Revelation expands upon the destruction of this rebellious creature in greater detail. It says he will be "tormented day and night forever and ever" (Revelation 20:10b). No wonder he's dreading his future. Apparently, the Old Testament verses describing his "destruction" do not mean that he ceases to exist, but that he is unable to cause any more trouble.

God will destroy the devil's power and influence over the lives of humans against whom he has been waging war. He will still exist, but he will be utterly impotent to harm us in any way. God will not annihilate the devil, but his kingdom will be utterly undone and destroyed. Satan's empire has a definite and permanent crushing end from which it will never rise again.

Who He's Not

Now that we understand a little better who our enemy is, we must also be certain of what he is not.

As a master of propaganda and a deceitful masquerader, he has quite successfully skewed our assumptions and impressions of him, all to his advantage, of course. He promotes and encourages falsehoods about his existence, nature, and power because he doesn't want us to know the truth about him.

1. He is not an equal opposing force.

God alone exists eternally uncreated. Every other being is part of His creation (Colossians 1:15-17). God created the angel who rebelled and became Satan; therefore, he cannot be equal with God. Satan is a superhuman spiritual being, but he is not divine. He never has been and never will be.

The Bible is clear that Christianity, unlike many other religions and philosophies, is not dualistic. There is no yin-yang balance of good and evil.

Neither are we dealing with two great equal but opposite powers fighting against each other, uncertain of who will gain the upper hand. Rather, this epic war is between One Great Power and one lesser created being that refuses to submit.

2. He is not the ruler of Hell.

The devil is not the master of the dominion of Hell as is commonly depicted in caricatures of him. Hell is Satan's prison—not his home, not his kingdom, never his to rule.

Hell is a place of "eternal fire prepared for the devil and his angels" (Matthew 25:41b). God didn't prepare this place for Satan and his fallen angels so they could have their own little corner of the universe to control. God created it, so He has a place to lock them all up when He decides their deceitful mutiny is finished for good (Revelation 20:10).

3. He is not all-knowing.

Satan is intelligent, but not omniscient. There's a whole lot he doesn't know. Don't listen to his lies. He acts like a know-it-all, but only God knows all (Romans 11:33-34). He cannot read our minds, know our thoughts, or search our hearts as God does (1 Kings 8:39).

However, having observed human responses and interactions for a few thousand years, he's probably learned a thing or two about how we tend to operate. He may not know what we're thinking, but he can make a calculated guess and formulate his schemes against us accordingly.

5. He is not all-powerful.

Satan is not omnipotent. Contrary to the popular excuse, the devil is powerless to *make* us do *anything*. He must get permission from God to intervene in our lives. And even then, we are agents of free will and fully capable of resisting him and saying, "No! I won't cooperate with your plan for my own undoing."

Evil can be powerful, but it is limited—contained within boundaries set by God. Our enemy is a growling dog with a nasty bite, but God has him on a sturdy leash designed for His good purposes.

In fact, God's word tells us to overcome evil with good (Romans 12:21). That is not possible unless God's goodness, kindness, and compassion are more powerful than evil, hatred, and fear. Everything that is good and right comes from God and dominates all the twisted and perverted lies of the enemy. The light of Truth overcomes the darkness of deceit (John 1:5, 2 Corinthians 4:6) and Jesus' righteousness has triumphed over sin and death (1 Corinthians 15:57, Colossians 2:15).

6. Neither is he powerless.

Although conquered, he is still dangerous. Peter describes him as a lion capable of devouring us (1 Peter 5:8). We are instructed to be on high alert because our enemy prowls among us and has the power to kill, steal, and destroy us, not because he is a tame kitten without fangs or claws. Never underestimate your opponent! That can be a deadly mistake.

7. He does not have creative powers.

God alone is the Creator. Only He can make something out of nothing (Hebrews 10:10-12).

Three times, Pharaoh's magicians replicated the miracles God did through Moses by using their "secret arts." They turned a staff into a snake, changed water to blood, and caused frogs to come up out of the waters—or at least they made it look like they did (Exodus 7-8).

Whether their "secret art" was some form of demonic counterfeit miracles or common slight-of-hand trickery, I don't know. But the interesting part is what they *couldn't* do.

The first time they failed to copycat Moses was when he struck the ground and produced a swarm of gnats. They were stumped. They could change the substance and form of what already existed, but they *could not* produce something out of nothing. The power to create is reserved for God alone. God is a Creator; Satan is a destroyer.

8. He is not fearless.

The powers of darkness and evil shudder in fear at even the thought of God (James 2:9), evidenced by the fearful response of demons to Jesus. "What do you want with us, Son of God?" they shouted. "Have you come here to torture us before the appointed time?" (Matthew 8:29)

Perhaps Satan knows so well how to use our fears against us because he is intimately familiar with the torment of his fears of his coming judgment and impending doom shadowing his miserable future. He seeks to spread his fear and gloom to us, but we must be sure that if we join with Jesus, we have a much different future awaiting us—one far more glorious and exquisite than we can possibly imagine.

"Satan trembles when he sees the weakest saint upon their knees."
~ William Cowper

The Next Step: Fight Back!

We need to understand that we are in a real battle against a real enemy, but know that our enemy is never other people. Our enemies are evil powers. We are called to resist the devil and love the people.

We must be careful to avoid the dangerous extremes of either ignoring Satan altogether or focusing on him, instead of keeping our attention fixed on Jesus.

We are better equipped to resist the enemy when we are familiar with his tactics. Yes, he is a defeated foe, but in his death throes, he is still a dangerous threat and a formidable adversary.

Our victory is in Christ alone, and it is only by His grace and power that we are victorious in our battles against the forces of darkness.

Now that we understand who our enemy is and what he wants, we must learn how to fight back through resistance. By recognizing his tactics and engaging our will to refuse to cooperate with his efforts, we will learn how to claim the victory that has already been won for us by Christ.

CHAPTER 6

THE REAL FIGHT:
RESIST YOUR ENEMY

Opposing Your Unrelenting Adversary

*"The spirit-to-spirit combat I endlessly wage with Satan is this fero-
cious thrash for joy. He sneers, at all the things that seem to have gone
mad in this sin-drunk world, and I gasp to say God is good. The liar
defiantly scrawls his graffiti across God's glory, and I heave to
enjoy God...and Satan strangles, and I whiten knuckles
to grasp real Truth and fix that beast to the floor."*
~ *Ann Voskamp*, One Thousand Gifts

Resisting Evil

Far from passive agents in this epic spiritual battle, we must learn to
push back the darkness if we want to enjoy the light of victory.

The Grocery Store: A Different Kind of Battlefield

Before I had any children, I would watch moms at the grocery store
with their young ones with fear and trepidation. Shopping with little
ones in tow seemed horribly slow and frustratingly difficult. I wondered how I would be able to manage such a task.

I vividly remember the first time I ever did a full-scale grocery
trip by myself with my newborn son. I did pretty well until we got to

the frozen section. At the first hint of a tiny cry, I panicked and fled to check out immediately for fear of becoming a public spectacle. This turned out to be a dumb thing to do because I had to go **back** to the store the next day to finish purchasing what we needed.

Eventually, I figured out how to shop with a baby and not come unglued at the first hint of trouble. Becoming a mother is accomplished primarily through on-the-job training and learning from our mistakes.

But then, we had another child.

When we were expecting our second baby, I wondered, "How will I ever do this with two?" But we managed. And then Baby Number Three was on the way. "Okay, two was manageable, but where do I put a third kid?"

And we didn't stop with three. One cartful was not enough. New babies kept coming every couple of years. I made it all the way up to shopping with six kids before I had one who was old enough to babysit the others while I ran to the store for diapers and milk.

As you can guess, grocery shopping with six children, from ages eleven and under, and two carts (pushing one and pulling the other) is a major event. Every other Friday, we made a day of running errands, a picnic lunch, and finished off with a trip to the commissary (a military grocery store).

It was actually kind of a fun day out of the house, which I didn't often do back then. I enjoyed the time I spent with my children and relished coming home to a clean house. (We hired a house cleaner during that busy season. That's **why** we stayed out of the house all day! Please don't think for a second I can "do it all." No one can but Jesus, and even He napped in the boat once in a while!)

Being a good military family, we always had a pre-brief in the car to discuss our mission before entering the ~~battlefield~~ grocery store. I would remind the children not to pull things off the shelves, not to beg for things that weren't on our already lengthy list, and for heaven's sake, **please** speak kindly to one another!

Trying to keep my speech light-hearted and "fun," I would often finish with my favorite question, "How do we walk down the aisles, children?"

"Like Sand People!" came the chorus from the full backseats of our minivan.

"That's right," I'd remind them ominously. "Sand People always ride single file to hide their numbers."

We didn't hide very well, but it was a memorable way to remind them not to take up the entire aisle and block the other shoppers from getting anywhere. Our mere presence alone already interrupted too many other shoppers who stopped to stare with gaping mouths while they indiscreetly counted my "troops."

(Umm . . . I can see your finger pointing at us and your lips mouthing numbers. You're not hiding from me by being quiet. The pale look of shock and awe on your face totally gives away what you think of my family. But that's okay, because I am blessed more abundantly than you can even imagine! Smile.)

Recognize Your Enemy

In *Star Wars*, the Sand People apparently had a trick they frequently employed to hide the strength of their troops and sneak up on whoever they were trying to attack. Obi-Wan was able to recognize their work and differentiate it from a Stormtrooper attack by observing the scene.

By correctly classifying the tactic used during the attack, he was able to discern who his true enemy was, thus preventing a pointless retaliation against the wrong enemy. Also, by knowing who his enemy was, he was able to figure out what they were after and how he should respond to the threat.

Just like Sand People who always ride single file, your enemy also has some consistent tactics to achieve his objectives. He is also a master of deception, making it appear that someone else is your enemy. He's like the Stormtroopers trying to pin his assault on the Sand People.

Be discerning. Learn to look at events in your life in a way similar to Obi-Wan. Is your current struggle caused by what or who you think it is, or could this be an enemy attack from the *real* dark side of spiritual forces?

You need to be able to point to the damage in your life and say, "And these blast points—too accurate for Sand People. Only Imperial Stormtroopers are so precise." In other words, this isn't mere carelessness or some mean person out to get me; this is the enemy trying to steer me off course or entrap me.

We can learn to recognize the devil's handiwork by identifying his tactics, which we will cover later in this chapter. Before we get to specific tactics, we need to analyze his overall objective and goals. We touched on this briefly in the previous chapter, but let's dig a little deeper now.

Your Enemy's Mission Objective

You son of the devil, full of every sort of deceit and fraud, and enemy
of all that is good! Will you never stop perverting
the true ways of the Lord?
~ Acts 13:10, NLT

To recognize the enemy's efforts to derail us, we must consider what his overall goal is and where he commonly takes aim to achieve that end.

What does he want anyway?

We have victory in Christ, but too often we leave it unclaimed.

The devil can't win. His original intent was to rise above God and usurp his throne. He lost that war. He knows it, and we know it (if you didn't skip Chapter 5!). He's already doomed. So, if his objective can't possibly be to win, what is it?

He knows his time is short and he's ticked off about it (Revelation 12:12). He's a sore loser, angry that God is still on the throne and he is not, so he retaliates on several fronts.

He attacks God's character.

He seeks to draw worship away from God and Jesus in particular who he especially hates. He succeeds in his objective through deceit. He makes his lies about God seem so true we willingly defect from God's sphere of blessing and protection.

He assaults God's people.

Misery loves company. So if the devil is doomed to lose, he at least wants to share the bitterness of his downfall with as many people as possible. He tries to do this by persuading us that we are defeated, when actually, he's the conquered one. We have victory in Christ, but too often we leave it unclaimed.

He attacks the people God has created and loves infinitely, all the while getting them to blame each other, or even better, to blame God for their problems, pain, and dissatisfaction.

He separates God's people from Jesus.

The devil's goal is to drive a wedge between God and us. God offers us the security of an eternal life in Paradise. The devil entices us away from perfection in glory to join him in misery and destruction.

He separates God's people from each other.

In sharing our common struggles, we are often encouraged and strengthened to carry on. We divide our burdens and multiply our joys when we share the load.

Our enemy wants us to believe we are isolated. We walk different journeys, but at our core, we all have the same root struggles in this life. We are never as alone as we feel. If we only muster the bravery to give voice to our inner selves authentically, we find that many others will respond with a whispered, "Me too. I thought I was the only one."

Satan can't win, but he *can* encourage us to lose. We must fight for our faith and forfeit no ground to his deceit and trickery.

His Favorite Targets

"The thief comes only to steal and kill and destroy; I have come that
they may have life, and have it to the full."
~ John 10:10, NIV

God has good plans for us, to give us abundant life and a hopeful future (Jeremiah 29:11, John 10:10). Unfortunately, sometimes the enemy remembers that fact even better than we do. Satan opposes the good plans God has for us, and he strives to undermine and snatch them away.

Satan's plans are *only* to steal, kill, and destroy. His promises are always hollow. Don't be fooled. His motive is always to use you, not make your life better in any way. He dangles shortcuts, easy wins, and self-indulgence before us, but it never quite turns out the way we expected because our expectations were not based on solid truth to begin with. Flirting with the devil's lies is always shaky ground.

To Steal

> *"Jesus once said that Satan was a thief. Satan does not steal money,*
> *for he knows that money has no eternal value. He steals only*
> *what has eternal value—primarily the souls of men."*
> ~ Zac Poonen

The devil is a master at taking what is rightfully ours and denying us our inheritance. He's not powerful enough to outright snatch it out from under us. But he can convince us it doesn't belong to us, or we don't want/need it, or we don't deserve it, or we are not good enough to take hold of it.

He can't steal it if we don't cooperate, so he lies to us. He sends his deceitful messages to us through advertisements, our culture, books, our friends, and thousands of other small and seemingly innocent ways.

- We let him steal our hope when we listen to his whispers that God's promises are untrue or not meant for us.

- He attempts to rob us of our peace by querying, "Can you *really* trust God to take care of you?"

- He puts a leak in our joy by tempting us to be dissatisfied and ungrateful.

- He undermines Jesus' overcoming power in us by telling us we're nothing but losers.

- He plunders our thanksgiving as he blinds us to the daily blessings God liberally pours out over us.

- He saps us of our strength, saying, "You aren't enough. You can't handle this."

- He tries to weaken our resolve with the message, "You'll never win."

- He tempts us to turn away when he deceives us into thinking God doesn't love or care about us.

To Kill

"Satan loves to attack before a venture for Christ and after a victory."
~ Ruth Myers

The devil is afraid of the great things God will do through His people, so he often threatens to take them out.

By killing, I don't just mean danger to our physical lives. It could refer to the death of a dream, or a relationship, or of our hope. Satan stands ready to gobble up whatever the Lord has birthed through us (Revelation 12:4b), whether that is a ministry, a marriage, or a message.

How many noted Christian leaders do you know who have fallen hard into a sinful lifestyle that surprised us all? Satan tries to kill God's message by shooting His messengers.

Praise God that even though the grass withers and the flowers fall, the word of our God endures forever (Isaiah 40:8). God's message, His good news of redemption and resurrection, can never be killed.

To Destroy

Sometimes, the devil doesn't try snatching it away or killing it completely; he just wrecks it, leaving a mangled mess of destroyed lives in his wake. If he can't take us out, he'll try to take us down.

He attempts to:

- destroy our hope
- cripple our faith
- shatter our dreams
- crush our hearts
- eat away at our minds
- deteriorate and deform our bodies
- deflate our will
- terrorize us with overinflated fears
- neutralize our power
- undermine our ministry
- wreck our family
- muck up our marriage
- entice our children to wander off in the serving of self

The Best News we have here is that there is nothing God can't redeem. He won't always restore things to the way they were, but He will make us better and bless us more, even in the midst of our mess. But we have to listen to God and tune out the devil to make that happen.

Be Alert

Be alert and of sober mind. Your enemy the devil prowls around like a roaring lion looking for someone to devour. Resist him, standing firm in the faith, because you know that the family of believers throughout the world is undergoing the same kind of sufferings.
~ 1 Peter 5:8-9, NIV

God's holy words warn us to be alert and to know the devil's schemes, so our enemy will not outwit us (2 Corinthians 2:11). The enemy will overcome us much easier if we are unaware and unprepared, and our ignorance will allow him to take us down or take us out of the fight—as a casualty or a POW.

If God tells us to know something, then it must be knowable. He doesn't ask us to do the impossible. (That's His job.) Let's examine our enemy's favorite tactics, so we know what to look for.

Be Aware of His Schemes

Anyone you forgive, I also forgive. And what I have forgiven—
if there was anything to forgive—I have forgiven in the sight of
Christ for your sake, in order that Satan might not outwit us.
For we are not unaware of his schemes.
~ 2 Corinthians 2:10-11, NIV

Whether it's an armed conflict, a football game, or any confrontation you hope to win, the plan is generally to strike where your opponent is weak. There are weaknesses inherent in all humanity, and we each have our own trouble spots as well. Our enemy has been studying humans for thousands of years, and he knows the areas where we tend to trip.

We must learn how to recognize the tactics of the enemy if we wish to avoid them. Ignorance may be bliss, but it is not victorious. You can't ignore or turn your back on your enemy without risking injury, capture, or death. You don't want to be a casualty in the fight for your faith.

> We must learn how to recognize the tactics of the enemy if we wish to avoid them. Ignorance may be bliss, but it is not victorious.

That's probably why you picked up this book in the first place—because you don't want to feel defeated anymore. If we know Satan's schemes, we can learn to identify when he is at work in our attitude or circumstances.

The devil is a formidable enemy, but he is not very creative. God alone has unlimited creativity. The enemy will keep using the same tactics over and over as long as they keep working. So quit falling for them and refuse to play along with his dangerous games.

We ought to use his lack of creativity to our advantage. It makes it much easier to discern his tactics when he doesn't change them very much. The element of surprise is an effective tactic in military operations. If we are aware of how he operates, he loses that advantage over us.

So what is the devil's game plan? How does he think? What is his plan for keeping us defeated?

Sun Tzu was an acclaimed military general, strategist, and philosopher who lived in China approximately 500 years before Christ. Military professionals study his writings even today. His tactics for overcoming an enemy sound very much like what our enemy tries to do to us.

"When the enemy is relaxed, make them toil. When full, starve them. When settled, make them move. When strong, avoid them. If of high morale, depress them. Seem humble to fill them with conceit. If at ease, exhaust them. If united, separate them. Attack their weaknesses. Emerge to their surprise. So in war, the way is to avoid what is strong, and strike at what is weak."
~ *Sun Tzu,* The Art of War

Our enemy always strikes us when we are weak, unsuspecting, and undefended. That's what enemies do. Being alert and ready, armed with a basic knowledge of his schemes and a plan to avoid them, makes it much more difficult for him to strike at us effectively.

Five Parts of Personhood

May God himself, the God of peace, sanctify you through and through.
*May your whole **spirit**, **soul** and **body** be kept blameless*
at the coming of our Lord Jesus Christ.
~ *1 Thessalonians 5:23, NIV (emphasis mine)*

The human battle against the onslaught of evil is a multi-front war. There are five main areas of our lives we need to fortify against his attacks.

We are composed of three parts—our spirit, soul, and body (1 Thessalonians 5:23).

- Your **spirit** is the part of you that relates to God and lives forever—from conception to eternity.

- Your **soul** also has three parts. It is your immaterial personhood consisting of your **mind**, **will**, and **emotions**. It is your essential being and what makes you uniquely you. While each has unique aspects, the mind, will, and emotions also overlap quite a bit. There is not always a clearly defined line where one ends and another begins.

- Your **body** is the container that carries around your spirit and soul while you live on earth. Our bodies are frail and temporary vessels while we walk this earth, but our eternal, heavenly, resurrected bodies will be imperishable and perfected clothed in glory and power (1 Corinthians 15:35-58).

Altogether, this makes five parts of our being that work together in very intricate and interconnected ways. None of these parts are completely independent. Strength or weakness in any area affects the condition of all the other areas to varying degrees.

1. Spirit
2. Mind
3. Will
4. Emotions
5. Body

Because our spirit is the part that most directly communes with God and is connected to His power, it is the dominant component. A strong spirit can override weakness in the other areas. Likewise, we can never compensate for a weak spirit by strength in every other area.

These parts of ourselves are constantly under attack from the devil and must be protected by the power of Christ. Our enemy's assaults will strike where we are weak via every opportunity we leave unfortified. Therefore, we must stand strong in our spirit, mind, will, heart, and body.

1. Spirit: He seeks the opportunity to attack our spirits.

Since our spirits are the part of us that abides with God, if he can successfully hit us here, he will generate maximum impact thus weakening us everywhere. There are many subtle ways he attempts to damage our relationship with God. He lures us with idolatry, puffs up our pride, attacks our obedience, and promotes hypocrisy, to name a few.

2. Mind: He tries to twist our thoughts and steal the truth from us.

The battleground for the war on truth is in our minds. We must be vigilant not to give up any ground nor lose any territory in the kingdom of Truth, for it is only in The Way, The Truth, and The Life that our victory lies (John 14:6).

Our adversary:

- Lies incessantly
- Makes lies seem perfectly reasonable
- Makes sin appear harmless
- Conceals true intentions
- Falsely accuses and condemns us
- Fuels and inflates our fears

3. Will: He attempts to assault our will to keep fighting the good fight by fueling propaganda.

Another sneaky way the devil tries to "win" is by causing us to forfeit. The truth is not on his side. All he's got are lies and propaganda, because the truth is that he's already defeated.

He distorts the truth and makes . . .

- the obstacles loom larger
- our fears seem scarier
- our resources look more limited
- our abilities feel more diminished
- and our God appear farther away

. . . than what is actually true.

He does all he can do to dilute our resolve, so we will want to quit, give up, and give in. Persevering until the very end denies the devil this false victory.

4. Emotions: He drives us hard to discourage us and lead us down the road of despair.

Because our thoughts and emotions are intimately connected, the way we think affects the way we feel. And the way we feel can enhance or distort our thoughts. Both of these together influence the way we interact with God and with others.

It is possible to *feel* defeated even when we are winning. Sometimes, our enemy lies to us through our feelings even more than he does through our minds. It all depends on where we are weakest at that moment.

A very common and effective way the enemy discourages us is by breeding discontent. Thanklessness leaves us restless and dissatisfied, always wanting a little something more but not quite sure what it is.

5. Body: He tries to diminish our effectiveness in service and enjoyment of life by encouraging the neglect or abuse of our bodies.

Once again, the devil can't destroy us himself unless God allows it, but he is often successful at talking us into destroying ourselves. He has many avenues through which he attacks us by way of our choices and habits.

- addictions

- eating disorders
- eating non-nourishing "food"
- self-loathing
- self-harm
- suicidal thoughts and attempts
- unhealthy habits
- physical inactivity
- stress
- sleeplessness
- risky behaviors
- neglecting self-care

Living in opposition to God's will for our lives is hard on our bodies. When our bodies are damaged or diseased, it can have a negative impact on our desire and ability to serve others.

Of course, as we already discussed in Chapter 2, not all physical ailments are an indication of evil happenings. Sometimes, like the blind man of John 9, God wishes to use our limitations for His glory.

But we must also remember that illness and injury entered the world via the open door of sin. Neither spiritual nor physical distress is God's ultimate best and highest for us.

Physical impairment is not always cut and dry, but we do know that God wants us to take good care of the bodies He's gifted us with regardless of our present level of physical health. Whatever degree of bodily well-being and fitness you possess, thank God for it and use it for His glory.

It's not the number of talents, but what you do with what you've got that matters. There's no excuse for neglecting, burying, or abusing what God has entrusted to you for His Kingdom work. (Read Jesus' *Parable of the Talents* in Matthew 25:14–30).

So Much More!

There is a lot that I desire to share about how these five areas of our being can be strengthened for God's glory or weakened to the devil's delight. In fact, I have so much more to tell you on this topic that it has become a whole separate book!

The second book in the STAND STRONG series is called *UNDAUNTED: Your Battle Plan for Victorious Living*. This daily battle plan will equip you with practical steps and tools to strengthen each of these five key areas of your life.

I have been using the strategies I share in the book regularly for over five years, and it has made a colossal difference in my life. I still have moments and days when I feel discouraged or defeated, but now I usually know what to do about it and how to shift my focus back to God's goodness and greatness more quickly.

Resist the Devil

"Experience teaches us that it is much easier to prevent an enemy from posting themselves than it is to dislodge them after they have got possession."
~ George Washington

As we've seen, Satan has a battle plan against us. Now we need a plan to counter it. God has provided all we need to live a victorious godly life. He has written our plan of resistance in His Word. It's time to push back.

Submit yourselves, then, to God. Resist the devil, and he will flee from you. Come near to God and he will come near to you.
~ James 4:7-8a, NIV

During basic training, we were assigned shifts to guard the entrance to the camp in Jack's Valley where we lived in tents for a couple of weeks. We were handed a rubber M-16 and ordered to stand in a tiny guard shack by the gate.

The running joke was that if any unauthorized person tried to access the camp, our response would be, "Stop! Or...I'll say stop again!" Our "weapons" were completely ineffective, and we all knew it. We had no authority, no power, and only a toy gun to dissuade any would-be infiltrators from gaining entry to our "stronghold."

Is this how you feel when faced with the evil in the world around you? No power, no authority, and nothing with which to fight back?

Do you feel like the enemy has invaded your territory and there's nothing you can do about it but throw your hands up and pray for an immediate rapture? That's exactly how the devil wants you to feel, but it's not true.

- **We possess the power.** God is all-powerful, and He shares with His followers. The same power that raised Jesus from the dead lives in us (Romans 8:11, Ephesians 1:19). This power in us is greater than any power at work in the world around us (1 John 4:4).

- **We have the authority.** Jesus told us the very gates of Hell cannot withstand His believers. (Matthew 16:18, 18:18). We are first and foremost under God's authority, but when we are acting in accordance with His will, we can be confident that He is working through us (Titus 2:15, 1 Peter 4:11, 2 Corinthian 5:20).

- **We've got effective weapons.** God has already given us everything we need for godly living (1 Peter 1:3). If He has told us to resist the enemy, then He will also equip us to do so. He enables us to demolish strongholds and capture ungodly thoughts that seek to anchor themselves within our minds (2 Corinthians 10:4). We will take a look at our weapons later in Chapter 10.

The problem is that too often, we are unaware of our power and authority. We treat our weapons of warfare as mere plastic toys—ornaments to help us play the part, but ineffective to defeat the foe. We have all we need to tell the enemy, "You can't come here," but how often do we do it?

Remember what we learned in the last chapter? Your enemy is not all-powerful. The devil can't *make* you do anything. God gave you a free will, and He is rooting for you to choose wisely when you decide who to listen and follow. We **can** push back successfully. In fact, that's what we're supposed to do.

Our enemy's greatest power lies in the human moral weakness that results when we fail to abide with God. Spiritual weakness impairs our ability to resist the subtleties of evil as we have been instructed to do. It is our pride that mirrors his, our lack of love for God and people, and our selfish disobedience that gives the devil any power at all.

He can only take what we give over to him. When we lay claim and hold on tight to our inheritance in Christ, running boldly to the throne of grace (Hebrews 4:16), he cannot defeat us nor steal what is rightfully ours in Christ.

We are rescued from the dominion of darkness, and we now belong to Jesus' kingdom of light (Colossians 1:12-13). We must choose to walk daily in the freedom that is already ours.

> *"No weapon forged against you will prevail, and you will refute every tongue that accuses you. This is the heritage of the servants of the LORD, and this is their vindication from me," declares the LORD.*
> *~ Isaiah 54:17, NIV*

We have to continue to resist him actively. The good news is that when we push back, he runs off. To resist him effectively, let us ask ourselves, "How can I make it more difficult for my enemy to harass and defeat me? How can I use what I've learned about his tactics to defend and protect myself from his threats?"

The Day I Learned to Resist

During basic training at the Academy, we went through the Assault Course, which is an obstacle course with an attitude. The obstacles were designed with a battlefield mindset.

We crawled under barbed wire and hurled pinecone "grenades" at imaginary enemies. They also trained us in close combat tactics and bayonet use. . . Because, you know, it's important for people in the Air Force to be prepared to use bayonets.

We all carried World War II-era M1 rifles into this simulated combat zone. The barrels had been filled with lead to prevent anyone from actually firing a projectile. We were told in no uncertain terms to never, under any circumstances, surrender our weapons to the enemy.

There is a great paradox at the Academy. The upperclassmen play the part of both the "enemy," who we are taught to resist at all cost, and the "commanding officer" who we are to obey without hesitation or question. Needless to say, it can sometimes get confusing when to resist and when to submit.

So they had worked out a code to differentiate their actions, attempting to make it clearer. If an upperclassman growled, "Give me your gun," or tried to take it from us physically, we were to resist as if our life depended on it.

But if moments later the same upperclassman said, "Surrender your weapon," then that meant, "No, really. I'm giving you a direct order. Obey me and hand it over. I want to teach you something."

No Mercy

Almost immediately upon arriving at the Assault Course the first time, I was pulled aside and escorted into the forest by a couple of upperclassmen. Out of earshot and visual range of anyone else, they were free to harass me without any oversight or interference.

When the more antagonistic of the two upperclassmen grabbed my weapon and asked me to give it to him, I mistakenly thought he was playing the role of "commanding officer." I released my grip and let him have it.

That was the moment all hell broke loose upon me.

He began to rant and scream about what a horrible excuse for a soldier I was, just handing my gun over to the bad guys like that. His bullying intensified tenfold as punishment for my heinous crime.

He was merciless.

He drove me to my absolute limits physically while he simultaneously spewed a hateful and endless barrage of insults highlighting my obvious failures as a human being. I made a grievous error in judgment because I thought my "enemy" was trying to teach me something. It turns out, his goal was to trick me, so he could claim the right to beat me.

After my squadron had completed running through the Assault Course, he released me to rejoin them.

The second phase of our training at the A-Course involved instruction in close combat with a weapon that was apparently out of ammo. We became semi-experts in using our firearms to cause blunt force trauma and destruction to our foes.

They taught us to thrust and parry with our imaginary bayonets. We also practiced various "butt-strokes" to incapacitate someone without shooting them by using the non-shooting end of the gun. (Good to know when you need to conserve bullets.)

The Power of No

We had to visit the Assault Course multiple times, and every time, I was immediately pulled aside by my two personal trainers and escorted back into our little private spot in the forest, out of sight of anyone who had the power to stop the abuse.

After putting up with this harassment for several hours over a number of days, Cadet Bully tried again to take my weapon away by force. But after enduring his wrath for so long, I was in no mood to repeat my former mistake.

I was ready for him this time. With an "Oh, no you don't!" attitude, I yanked my weapon away from his grip a little harder than necessary, inadvertently bringing it up over my left shoulder.

This position happened to be the way we initiated the maneuver that had just recently been drilled into my muscle memory called "butt smash to the head." And in that moment of desperation, that was all I could think about . . . How badly did I want to drive the butt end of my rifle into my tormentor's skull.

I was angry and fed up with his intimidation tactics and belittling barrage of insults. It took every last ounce of willpower I possessed not to strike him as hard as I could. My determination and inward struggle to not retaliate must have shown itself in my face because the upperclassman took a step back to put more distance between us.

I regret to say that a sense of satisfaction washed over me when I saw the fear in his eyes. Somehow, in the flash of a moment, we communicated without a word. He got my message of "don't mess with me anymore" loud and clear and he backed down.

Either he figured I had learned my lesson, decided I was tougher than I looked at first glance, or he just lost interest when I stood up to him. I'm not sure. We never spoke about it, and I never saw him again. He just let me go.

I completed basic training without actually running the Assault Course, yet still managing to learn the lesson the course was designed to teach me. I discovered that I had within me the ability to assault someone if it was necessary and right.

The only thing that held me back that day was a clear conscience in the midst of my rattled emotions and fatigued body, but if my cause had been just, I'm confident that guy would have **at least** been seriously injured by my hand.

That was a defining moment of my life. I learned the power of my own "No."

Just Say "No!"

As Christians, our "No" also carries power. We don't have to lay ourselves down and take being beaten by the enemy. By God's grace and through His power, we can stand strong and fight back. Say, "No" to your enemy and "Yes" to your God.

Never allow the enemy to take your weapons away thereby limiting your ability to fight the good fight God has set before you. Don't believe the enemy when he acts like you have no choice or that he's trying to help you.

Instead of going along with the enemy's suggestions and falling for his tricks, let us ask ourselves, "What does God want for me?" Choose God's best for you and reject evil. Don't give in. Hold on tight to all that God has given and ordained for you. Hold on tight and jerk it back with all your might.

Sometimes, you have to get a little angry with righteous anger. It's okay to get fed up with your enemy taking and killing and wrecking all that God intends to be beautiful in your world. Take it back by the power of the cross of Christ.

You, dear children, are from God and have overcome them [ungodly
spirits], because the one who is in you is greater than
the one who is in the world.
~ 1 John 4:4, NIV

Turn to the Light

Learn to live in the light of God's love. The darkness has no power over the light. Bathe your mind in the truth of God's word daily so that you will not be easily deceived. Know the truth so you can spot the counterfeit.

> *The light shines in the darkness, and the darkness has not overcome it.*
> *~ John 1:5, NIV*

Expose everything to the light of God's Truth. When we expose the subtle deceit the Father of Lies whispers and replace them with Truth, he loses his power to devour us. We are no longer tangled up in the traps, snares, and nets our enemy has laid out for us. God's Truth sets us free to fight our battles well and bring glory to God.

Overcome Evil with Good

> *Don't let evil conquer you, but conquer evil by doing good.*
> *~ Romans 12:21, NLT*

God's goodness triumphs over evil every time. When in doubt, do the next right thing in God's eyes. The enemy may have schemes for you, but God has plans for you that are far more powerful than any tactic the devil can conceive. Trust God's plans and power more than you fear the enemy's traps and tricks.

> Trust God's plans and power more than you fear the enemy's traps and tricks.

> *We know that God's children do not make a practice of sinning, for*
> *God's Son holds them securely, and **the evil one cannot touch them.***
> *We know that we are children of God and that the world*
> *around us is under the control of the evil one.*
> *~ 1 John 5:18-19, NLT (emphasis mine)*

Do the Opposite

Do not give the devil a foothold.
~ Ephesians 4:27, NIV

Don't give your enemy a foothold or even so much as a place to rest his little toe in your life. Oppose your opponent by doing the opposite. (See how those words are all closely related?)

When life spins sideways and situations start going off the rails, I have difficulty figuring out what God wants me to do. Sometimes we take a tumble and become so disoriented that it's hard to figure out which way is up.

When the right course of action isn't obvious, or I'm starting to feel defeated, I imagine what my enemy would want me to do and then I do the opposite.

- So when the devil wants me to give up, I'll keep marching on.

- When he tempts me to fight people instead of him, I'll give people a gentle answer and him an icy stare.

- When he pushes me to get ahead of God, I'll wait patiently and expectantly for God's perfect timing.

- When he suffocates me under the pressure of various trials, I'll focus on breathing deeply of God's Spirit of power and courage and love (2 Timothy 1:7).

- When he tries to put out the fire within me with buckets of cold water, I will fan the flame of God's good gifts (2 Timothy 1:6).

- When he brings up my past, I'll remind him of his future.

- When he drags me into a pit of discouragement, depression, or despair, I will call out to the One who lifts me up and sets my feet on solid ground (Psalms 40:2).

- When he assaults me with fear, I will cast all my anxieties upon Jesus who cares for me (1 Peter 5:7).

- When he tries to rile me, I will remain calm and unruffled, resting in Jesus who is my Prince of Peace (Ephesians 2:14, Isaiah 9:6).

- When he slings his fiery darts at me, I will raise high my shield of faith and press on to fight in the shade (Ephesians 6:16).

- When he feeds me lies, I will spit them out and consume the truth of God's Word.

- When he wants me to tremble in trepidation, I will choose to stand strong boldly with a heart of courage.

- When he attempts to silence me, I will praise God all the more.

- When he tries to stare me down, I will fix my gaze on Jesus alone.

- When he wants to fuel the fires of hate, I will respond with the cleansing waters of compassion.

- When he pours worries down upon me, I will lift up my eyes and worship the Lord of All.

- When he tells me I'm unloved, I will know I am God's Beloved.

- When he says I am defeated, I will shout that Jesus is my Victor and my Champion.

- When he wins a battle or two, I'll remember he's already lost the war.

- When he says I'm inadequate or not enough, I'll say Jesus is my All in All. He is always My More-Than-Enough.

- When he tempts me to self-pity, I will reach out to serve others in Jesus' name.

- When he makes me feel alone and abandoned, I will know that Jesus lives in me and my very own body houses the Holy Spirit of my God (1 Corinthians 6:19). My God is closer to me than my next breath. If I stretch out my hand to find Him, I have reached too far.

- When he says I'm worthless, I'll remind him of the price Jesus paid for me (1 Peter 1:18-19).

- When he whispers in the dark, "God doesn't love you," I will shout back, "God loved me so much that He gave His Best and His Only for me." (John 3:16)

What do you think the enemy would love for you to do right now? Get up and go do the opposite. Resist him and he'll leave. Live like you are undefeated and you will be!

Who Will Give Up First?

God will never give up on you. No matter how many times you resist Him, He will keep loving you and offer an eternal, abundant life to you.

Your enemy is not as committed as your God. When he sees he's not making any headway with you, he will give up and get lost. He will wait for a more opportune time (Luke 4:13). Just keep saying no. Keep resisting. Keep refusing to give in. Make sure the devil gives up before you do. After all, God is on your side.

If God is for us, who can be against us?
~ Romans 8:31b, NIV

The best news of all is that you are not in this fight alone. Jesus' victory on the cross over sin and death had already determined the outcome. Let's turn our attention now to our unbeatable God who fights for and through us to conquer everything that tries to crush or confound us.

CHAPTER 7

THE ONLY VICTOR: KNOW YOUR GOD

Knowing Your Invincible Champion

"You can have all the right notions in your head without ever tasting in your heart the realities to which they refer; and a simple Bible reader and sermon hearer who is full of the Holy Spirit will develop a far deeper acquaintance with his God and Savior than a more learned scholar who is content with being theologically correct."
~ J.I. Packer, Knowing God

Knowing vs. Knowing About God

"Jesus always wears white, and no matter what He does,
He never gets dirty."
~ elizabeth meyers, age 5

Knowing someone is different from knowing *about* someone. When we say we "know" a celebrity or famous person, we usually mean we know who they are. We recognize the name and can recall projects on which they've worked. We may even know some of their life story or personal life, but none of that is from firsthand knowledge. We've read about them, watched them on a screen, or heard them on the radio, but that doesn't mean we know them.

The people I know best are the ones I live and work with every day. The ones with whom I share my home, my meals, my inner thoughts—the personal spaces of my life.

To know someone deeper than a superficial level, we must spend time with, talk to, listen to, laugh with, and grow with them. The people we have the deepest bonds with are those with whom we've shared our greatest joys and worst struggles—the ones we walk with every day.

It is no different with God. He can either be a celebrity you only know about, or He can be the One you know more intimately than anyone else. He already knows you inside and out better than you even know yourself. You can't change that. But you do get to decide how well you know Him.

You decide if you just peruse the sensationalized tabloid headlines of what others spout about Him or if you spend personal, intimate time with Him on a daily, moment-by-moment basis. Though He is always with you, it is up to you whether you are aware of His presence in every moment, only when you're in great need, or not at all.

And this is the way to have eternal life—to know you, the only true
God, and Jesus Christ, the one you sent to earth.
~ John 17:3, NLT

The Goodness and Greatness of God

God is mighty, but despises no one.
~ Job 36:5a, NIV

A great and mighty god who was not holy would be a terrifying tyrant. A kind and loving god who was not all powerful would be impotent to accomplish the good he desired for us. Neither of these "gods" would be worthy of our worship. Like the mythological gods of old, they are too much like us (selfish and weak) to be elevated above us.

Fortunately, we don't have to settle for either of these pathetic options. We have a God who is both good and great.

God is Good and Present

Therefore, since we have a great high priest who has ascended into heaven, Jesus the Son of God, let us hold firmly to the faith we profess. For we do not have a high priest who is unable to empathize with our weaknesses, but we have One who has been tempted in every way, just as we are—yet He did not sin. Let us then approach God's throne of grace with confidence, so that we may receive mercy and find grace to help us in our time of need.
~ Hebrews 4:14-16, NIV

God is perfectly holy—without fault, stain, or blemish. Everything He does is superior in every way.

God always does the right thing because His actions are an extension of His love. It is love for us that also draws Him to be present with us.

Long ago, when Esther went to visit King Xerxes (who was also her husband), she feared for her life. She was supposed to report in only when summoned, but she was not permitted to initiate a meeting with the king (Esther 4:10-11).

Before she appeared to request help, she fasted for three days in preparation, praying that the king would choose to extend his golden scepter to spare her life. King Xerxes was only an earthly human king and not a very righteous one at that.

Can you imagine if approaching God were like that? What if we had to risk our lives and hope for a little mercy to request help from God?

Thankfully, Jesus is our personal Ambassador to God, so we can initiate an audience with the King of Kings without putting our lives at stake. He welcomes us into His presence with a loving embrace.

In His goodness, God is always available to us.

God is Great and Preeminent

*The heavens praise your wonders, Lord, your faithfulness too, in the
assembly of the holy ones. For who in the skies above can compare
with the Lord? Who is like the Lord among the heavenly beings? In
the council of the holy ones God is greatly feared; he is more awesome
than all who surround him. Who is like you, Lord God Almighty?
You, Lord, are mighty, and your faithfulness surrounds you.*
~ Psalm 89:5-8, NIV

By God's words, all things come into being, and by His breath they
are sustained or destroyed. He always has been and always will be,
existing uncreated and self-sustaining, depending on no one and
nothing. There is no weakness, blind spot, or infirmity of any kind
within Him.

All His thoughts are pure genius. He is beyond exceptional and
without equal. There are none who even come close to His match-
less wisdom. Overflowing with abundance, He is always more than
enough. He is Almighty. Anything is possible for Him. He shrouds
Himself in unapproachable light—unreachable and untouchable by
any other being.

The Ageless One, He is immortal and eternal, without beginning
or end. Though invisible and unseen, He is entirely indispensable.
Far beyond the reach of our comprehension, His ways and plans are
higher than we can ever fathom.

He is sovereign, the rightful ruler over everything and the loving
Lord of our lives. He alone is worthy of our worship and unconditional surrender.

The Battle Belongs to the Lord

How often do we feel defeated because we are taking ownership of a
battle that is not ours? We are striving hard against a foe we were not
meant to face alone, and we keep coming up short. What if we let
God handle our battles and rested in His victory, trusting His ability
to prevail? What peace do we pass up because we are struggling with
the crushing burden of our sin long after Jesus said, "It is finished"?

The Battle is Not Ours

Do not be afraid or discouraged because of this vast army.
For the battle is not yours, but God's.
~ 2 Chronicles 20:15, NIV

Guess what, folks. It's not up to us to win the war. We don't have to save the world. God already did that.

Sometimes we feel defeated because we're fighting a battle God never intended us to fight. A lot of times, He could handle all our situations much better if we'd just get out of His way.

I clean the kitchen ten times faster and better if I do it myself than if I try to get the kids to help me. Sometimes their "help" is most unhelpful, know what I mean?

And yet, I'm silly enough to think I can help God clean up my messes better than He can. *"If You'd just do XYZ, everything would be so much better, God. Thanks!"* Like He needs my input.

More than once in history, God told His people to sit tight and watch Him work. Can you imagine if the Israelites started making buckets to help God move the water of the Red Sea out of their way? Ridiculous! Nope. Nothing to do there but stand back and watch God do what only God could do.

Don't be afraid. Just stand still and watch
the LORD rescue you today.
~ Exodus 14:13, NLT

We get a front row seat to watch God move on our behalf, but we'll miss out on the joy and the peace if we're too busy with our buckets trying to do God's job for Him.

What victory in your life can God alone bring about? Are you ready to get out of His way and watch what He will do for you?

The War Is Already Won

No, despite all these things, overwhelming victory
is ours through Christ, who loved us.
~ Romans 8:37, NLT

Spoiler alert! Our victory has already been secured for us through the work of Jesus. We hold the winning lottery ticket, but we still have to claim our prize to receive the riches that belong to us.

Life is not a nail-biter, wondering if God and His angels or Satan and his forces of darkness will be victorious. God has already told us the ending, and He knew how it would all go down before it ever got started (Isaiah 46:10).

Jesus' heroic rescue of humanity was not God's "Plan B" after things went unexpectedly awry in Paradise. God planned to save us before He even created us, because He foresaw the trouble we would get ourselves into much like we often do for our children. When was the last time you had to bite your tongue to squelch the "I told you so" rising from within?

If we are to live victoriously, we must choose to be convinced that God has already earned the victory for us. It's not up to us to secure the victory. We must simply show up and claim the victory that has already been won for us. To do that, however, we must believe that we have the right to claim it.

We reap the benefits of what Jesus has already accomplished. We are the raving fans in the stands. Jesus is the player on the field with the winning score.

We are the average civilian unaware of what our freedom truly costs. Jesus is the Special Ops warrior swiftly taking down the enemy and purchasing our freedom with His blood.

When Evil is Undone

The reason the Son of God appeared was to destroy the devil's work.
~ 1 John 3:8b, NIV

Though the devil is frantically working to wreak as much havoc as possible upon God's beloved, ultimately, the work of Christ will make all his efforts unfruitful. You may feel undone today, but in the end it is Satan's work that will be undone and we who have trusted Jesus will be made whole.

Our enemy can harass us, but if we are connected with Jesus, he will have no permanent wins against us. We may walk away with a few battle scars, but we will leave this earth victorious if we choose to be on God's side.

Consider Jesus' dear friend Lazarus. He became deathly ill, but Jesus waited until he died to visit him. Jesus told His disciples that Lazarus' sickness would not end in death, which is ironic considering Lazarus was probably already dead when He made that statement (John 11:4).

> Because of Jesus, the devil's victory is short-lived, and we slip right through his fingers. Our victory in Christ is permanent and irreversible.

How can Jesus say death wouldn't be the end when Lazarus did, in fact, die? Because Jesus sees past the illness to the resurrection beyond. Mary and Martha thought the death of their brother was the end—a period. But all the while, God intended it to be only a comma preceding His unimaginable miracle.

Death may claim us, but it can't keep us. Because of Jesus, the devil's victory is short-lived, and we slip right through his fingers. Our victory in Christ is permanent and irreversible.

Who Gets the Glory?

All those gathered here will know that it is not by sword or spear that
the LORD saves; for the battle is the LORD's.
~ 1 Samuel 17:47a, NIV

When we act like it's all up to us to save the day, we only exhaust ourselves with burdens we weren't meant to carry. One of two things will probably happen. We will either push through to find some degree of success which others may attribute to our talent or perseverance (and we might happen to agree with them). Or, we will crash and burn, bemoaning the agony of defeat and wondering why we can never win.

We need to remember two things:

1. It's not our battle.
2. We're not supposed to get the glory for any wins.

When we live like the battle belongs to the Lord and not us, He gets the glory for winning the war. And isn't that our chief aim and purpose in life—to bring glory to God by how we live?

If you tend to swing erratically between feelings of pride and failure, check your attitude and see if maybe you think it's your battle. Let God fight the battle and give Him all the credit when He scores a win on your behalf.

> *The kingdom of Satan will surely fall before the kingdom of Christ,*
> *error before truth, profaneness before godliness, and corruption*
> *before grace in the hearts of the faithful.*
> *~ Matthew Henry*

Whose Side Are You On?

After the death of Moses, the Israelites crossed the Jordan River under Joshua's command and camped outside Jericho, which was the first place they had to conquer to claim what God had promised them.

One night, Joshua was alone near Jericho, presumably doing a little recon to establish a battle plan for attacking this heavily fortified city. As he surveyed the obstacle before him, he must have felt overwhelmed and perhaps a little defeated already.

It was here that Joshua looked up and saw a man with a drawn sword, indicating he was ready to fight. Unintimidated, Joshua stepped up to the man (who he later realized was God) and challenged him, asking, "Whose side are you on?" Joshua needed to identify if this guy was friend or foe (Joshua 5:13).

But Joshua's perspective was all wrong. He saw Jericho as his battle and the people and equipment in front of him as his resources. So Jesus showed up to straighten him out.

Jesus responded, "I'm not on either side. I'm the commander of the Lord's army, which is entirely independent of either of these two armies that square off on this battlefield today." (Joshua 5:14) Jesus did not show up to take sides, but to take control of the situation and set things right.

Joshua immediately acknowledged the Lord's right to direct the battle, and he put his face to the dirt in submission and worship. In an instant, he went from seeing himself as the general commanding officer to the foot soldier ready to take orders.

He stopped trying to formulate a plan of attack, and instead prepared to receive instructions for victory. He didn't say, "Well, here's what I've thought we should do, Lord. Please bless my plan." Whatever plans Josh had been formulating in his mind, he crumpled them up and tossed away. "What are my orders? What do *You* want me to do?" was his trusting response.

God's answer must have shocked him. There was no battle plan, no tactical training, and no insight into the secret weakness of the wall. There was only the direction to march around in silence until it was time to blow the trumpets with the priests (not the soldiers) leading the way.

Oh, how I wish I could've seen the look on Josh's face at that moment.

Do you think that maybe after Joshua heard God's idea for a battle plan, he was tempted to regret not voicing his plans earlier? Had I been the commanding officer and received orders from the Higher Up to lead the battle with the band, I would have thought, "Oh boy. I sure hope this guy knows what he's doing, or I'm going to look like a fool in front of the entire army and our enemies. We will become the laughing stock of the whole region, and no one will ever follow me anywhere again."

The Biblical account recorded the facts about the Lord's instructions and followed with Joshua passing on those instructions to the priests and the people. Then everybody obediently carried out the plan. This just-the-facts approach leaves out all the personal drama that I'm sure was a necessary part of this monumental event.

There's no record of what Joshua thought about the plan, or how he felt when he had to tell the others what they had to do. It doesn't mention any strange looks, eye rolls, talk of mutiny, opposition, or fringe groups with different plans. We are left to assume that everyone obediently and cheerfully cooperated with the strangest battle plan ever conceived.

That sounds nice, but we know humans. They don't work like that.

God has His reasons for leaving out the drama and focusing on the facts, but I can't wait to find Josh in Heaven someday and say, "So tell me what was going through your mind when you told the troops, 'Okay guys, here's what we're going to do to bring down the most heavily fortified city we've ever seen. . . Are your instruments in tune?" Talk about shock and awe!

God was showing them (and us) that it's His battle, and that He will win it with His plan (however quirky it may seem) and with His unlimited resources that we can't even imagine.

He's not on our side. We're on his side, but only if we choose to be. So I ask you now the same question Joshua asked the man-God he encountered, "Whose side are you on?"

Everyone has a choice. Even as God demonstrated His dominating power over the fortifications of Jericho, He showed His compassionate power to rescue anyone who desired to be rescued. God snatched Rahab and her family unharmed from the rubble of a fallen fortress and incorporated them into His victory march.

It was not because Rahab was nobler nor had more to offer than other inhabitants of Jericho. Her employment was more than a little sketchy and her big moment in Scripture largely consists of her deceptive techniques. It was simply because she believed God was who He said He was, and she willingly surrendered to Him.

I believe this same opportunity was available to all those who sought shelter within the city walls. She was just the only one recorded who took God up on His generous offer.

Those who depended on the fortifications of Jericho to protect them were destroyed that day, but all who depended on the Lord were spared, no matter from which side they originated.

If you realize you're living within the walls of "Jericho" but no longer wish to be there, turn to "Join the Victorious Kingdom Today!" in the resource section at the end of the book to see how you can trade the flimsy walls of this world for the sure defense of an unbeatable God.

Your Invincible Champion

God sent Jesus to win the war for you because He loves you. In Jesus, you are rescued, redeemed, secured, protected, defended, and empowered.

You are **rescued**. God *saves you because He cares for you.*
You are **redeemed**. God *delivers you because you can't free yourself.*
You are **secured**. God *holds you because He loves you.*
You are **protected**. God *shields you because He knows your weakness.*
You are **defended**. God *fights for you because the battle belongs to Him.*
You are **empowered**. God *fights through you because your weakness displays His strength.*

~~~~~

Rescued: *God saves you because He cares for you.*

We have already examined the victory Christ has won for us over sin and death. We were once slaves to sin and death, but now we have been rescued. He also continually saves us from earthly dangers both known and unknown.

Through Hell or High Water

Do not be afraid, for I have ransomed you. I have called you by name;
you are mine. When you go through deep waters, I will be with you.
When you go through rivers of difficulty, you will not drown. When
you walk through the fire of oppression, you will not be burned up;
the flames will not consume you. For I am the Lord, your God,
the Holy One of Israel, your Savior.
~ Isaiah 43:1b–3a, NLT

We do not need to fear the pain of the trials that befall us, for God has said, "When you walk through rough stuff, I'll be right there with you. You won't ever get burnt to a crisp or be in over your head if you stick with me."

Now, it may surely seem to us as though we are going under or being set ablaze, but He has promised to rescue us. That does not mean He will turn every circumstance in our favor or relieve us of every burden. But He has told us that these pains of earthly living are temporary.

Three times in the verse above, God says we will go ***through*** difficulties. First, He assures us that in this world we will have trouble (just in case we had any delusions of a care-free life). But in every instance, He promises we will go ***through*** the trials.

> *For our light and momentary troubles are achieving for us an eternal*
> *glory that far outweighs them all.*
> *~ 2 Corinthians 4:17, NIV*

We are not meant to stay stuck in a place of pain forever. He wants to guide us safely through to the other side. Like a young child who doesn't know the way, we can get lost and wander around in dark and lonely places if we stray too far from our Father.

When we find ourselves in places of suffering and panic, we must allow God to remind us that we are only passing through. This world and its heartbreak are not our Home. We are meant for Heavenly places of peace, perfection, comfort, and security. That is why this world is often so uncomfortable and unpleasant to us.

He has set Eternity within each human heart, and we constantly yearn for our True Home even though we may not be able to verbalize what we crave (Ecclesiates 3:11). Even our greatest trials and most gut-wrenching difficulties on this earth are light and momentary in contrast to the weight and expanse of the glory that awaits us.

Redeemed: *God delivers you because you can't free yourself.*

> *For the Lord is the Spirit, and wherever the Spirit of the Lord is,*
> *there is freedom.*
> *~ 2 Corinthians 3:17, NLT*

In this life, we encounter many forms of brokenness, tangled snarls of confusion, and messy-ugly situations that tempt us to lose hope. But there is nothing that is impossible for God to redeem.

There is no situation so messed up He can't blossom blessing from it. No person is so lost that God cannot find him. No act so evil that God cannot bring good from it. No loss so complete He cannot show us the path to victory.

When the enemy threatens to engulf us once again in slavery to his miserable tyranny, may we remember to run to Jesus in Whom our true freedom is found. Let us fortify our faith to stand strong by His power against the devil and his demons, knowing we never stand alone or in vain, certain that our God is able to:

- Redeem us from our slavery to sin and selfishness
- Resurrect whatever the enemy has killed
- Restore everything that has been stolen from us
- Rebuild the places in us that are wrecked and destroyed
- Replant the spiritual growth that has withered
- Re-energize us to be stronger than we were before
- Re-engage us to get us back in the fight
- Regain the territory we have surrendered to the enemy
- Rekindle the fires of godly passion
- Reignite the light of hope within us

And the God of all grace, who called you to is eternal glory in Christ,
after you have suffered a little while, will himself restore you and
make you strong, firm and steadfast. To him be the
power for ever and ever. Amen.
~ 1 Peter 5:10-11, NIV

Secured: *God holds you because He loves you.*

I give them eternal life, and they shall never perish;
no one will snatch them out of my hand.
~ John 10:28, NIV

Because our salvation did not require our righteousness to begin with, our security does not depend upon our ability or performance.

God holds us close even when we are too weak to hang on to Him. This is grace.

Secure for Eternity

God has a tattoo with your name on it. He has engraved your name on His hand (Is 49:16, NLT). He will never forsake you, and no one and nothing can ever pull you away or negate His love for you.

> *For I am convinced that neither death nor life, neither angels nor demons, neither the present nor the future, nor any powers, neither height nor depth, nor anything else in all creation, will be able to separate us from the love of God that is in Christ Jesus our Lord.*
> *~ Romans 8:38-39, NIV*

Having come out the other side of trauma I thought would end me, my message to you is this: God is faithful, even when we are not.

When I was unable and even unwilling to hold on to God in my darkest nights, He was still holding me though I could not perceive it at the time. Though I felt alone, He was always near. He acknowledged and saved every tear that fell from my shattered heart (Psalms 56:8, NLT).

I was numbed by my unbearable pain and blinded by my tears of grief. And yet, when the storm was over and the skies began to clear, there I was, safe in His grip the whole time.

My security in His grace was never dependent on the strength of my grip on Him. I was powerless to save myself in the first place. I am equally powerless to undo the eternal victory He has secured for me.

When I am crossing a dangerous street with my child, I do not depend on her ability to hold my hand. I hold hers—tightly. She may let go, but I will not, for I know the dangers that face her should we be separated, dangers she cannot even fathom nor comprehend, dangers she is powerless to save herself from.

> *For who is God besides the Lord? And who is the Rock except our God? It is God who arms me with strength and keeps my way secure.*
> *~ 2 Samuel 22:32-33, NIV*

Protected: *God shields you because He knows your weakness.*

But as for me, I will sing about your power. Each morning I will sing with joy about your unfailing love. For you have been my refuge, a place of safety when I am in distress.
~ Psalm 59:16, NLT

Soldiers must be shielded in order to advance. So seek God's protection as you move forward in whatever God has called you to do.

God's protection does not mean we will never face calamity. Our own attempts at righteousness do not earn us a free pass from pain. But we can be assured that any hardship that is allowed into our lives He has permitted for our ultimate gain.

Our God goes:

- Before us, as our Point-man
- Behind us, as our Rearguard
- Beside us, as our Shield

Before us, as our Point-man

I will go before you and make the rough places smooth
~ Isaiah 45:2, NASB

By laying down His life for us, He's already been to the Valley of Death ahead of us. He's conquered all the enemies that lurk there and is able to lead us through that same valley to the victory beyond.

Like a "point man" leading the way through danger, He clears the path before us. He has already "taken the bullet" for us, engaging the enemy's greatest assault and emerging the Victor. We need not fear to follow Him through any danger or shadowy descent. He will not lead us astray, but we must learn to stick close and follow well.

Behind us, as our Rearguard

Then your light will break forth like the dawn, and your healing will quickly appear; then your righteousness will go before you, and the glory of the Lord will be your rear guard. Then you will call, and the Lord will answer; you will cry for help, and he will say: Here am I.
~ Isaiah 58:8-9a, NIV

I know you've probably heard of the pillar of God's presence that led Moses and the people of Israel out of slavery and on their journey to freedom.

Not far into their freedom march, they came to a halt in front of their greatest obstacle yet. The sea was lapping at their feet, and the full force of the Egyptian army was coming up fast behind them. They were trapped. Then God moved.

The cloud that had been leading them up front relocated to a position behind the trembling Hebrews. They needed a guard more than a guide at this point. Their way ahead, an astonishing path through the sea, would soon be clear enough without the cloud to point the way. So God shielded them from their pursuers, giving every last Israelite time to cross over to victory.

When you can't sense God's leading or His comforting presence, look back at all that is behind and recount all the ways He has helped in the past. Maybe the cloud of His presence has moved to where you need it most right now.

Beside us, as our Shield

He will cover you with his feathers. He will shelter you with his wings. His faithful promises are your armor and protection.
~ Psalm 91:4, NLT

God is our living, loving, intelligent, and powerful shield. He is our hedge of protection the enemy cannot penetrate without His permission. There is no place we can run or fall that He can't reach us. No matter what battle we are facing today or will face soon, He is already there.

Our Heavenly Father is not far off, disengaged or uninterested. He is not standing over us with crossed arms and a scowling face. He is beside us—in the trenches of our daily struggles, shielding us from unseen dangers with His mighty hand and an outstretched arm (Psalms 136:12).

By His power, we can go stealth and drop off the enemy's radar. God can hide us under the shelter of His wings where we are safe and protected. Though a violent storm may rage, we can be at peace in the core of our being because He shields us from the impact of the blasts all around us.

However, He does not force Himself upon us uninvited. We must willingly enter the shelter He provides. Jesus ached for His people because He longed to gather them together and shield them as a hen does her chicks, but they were unwilling (Matthew 23:37, Luke 13:34). We have the option to refuse the shelter He provides, but we reject His shield to our peril.

Defended: *He fights for you because the battle belongs to Him.*

> *The LORD himself will fight for you. Just stay calm.*
> *~ Exodus 14:14, NLT*

I don't know about you, but I can get so wound up sometimes fighting for what I think is right or how it should be done and I hear God's gentle whisper, "Chill, Woman! If what you're striving for is My will, I can make it happen just fine without your help."

We certainly have a part to play, actions to take, and things that we must do. But our ultimate victory is because of God's power, used in God's way, in His perfect timing. We cannot manufacture nor generate victory for ourselves apart from God.

The Lord Is a Warrior

> *The LORD is a warrior; Yahweh is his name!*
> *~ Exodus 15:3, NLT*

God is not a pacifist or contentious objector when it comes to spiritual battles. He fights against evil for us on our behalf. He makes paths through the turbulent waters that threaten to engulf us, and extinguish the taunting cries of the armies of enslavement that rage against us.

He's our Lifeguard when we're drowning, our Policeman when we've been robbed, our Firefighter when our life is going up in smoke, our Medic when we lie wounded on the battlefield, our Bodyguard when we're threatened, our Search and Rescue when we've wandered astray and gotten lost, and our Liberator when we're in bondage. Whatever kind of Rescuer we need, HE IS.

When I saw the news footage of the Boston Marathon bombing, the thing that struck me most was the number of people who *immediately* ran *toward* the area where the bomb had just detonated.

Most people's first reaction would be to run the other way as fast as possible in case another bomb went off. But these people had no thought for their own safety. They saw wounded and desperate people, and with no regard for themselves, they were consumed by a single thought, "I have to help them."

That's how God sees us. He's the Hero that always runs toward the fight and into the disaster to rescue His beloved people. He never turns His back or looks away. God always heads toward us, intending to wrap His loving arms around us and soothe our broken spirits.

God has not left you to battle it out on your own. He didn't set the world in motion and walk away. He's right there in the thick of it with you. He fights for you.

I have told you all this so that you may have peace in me. Here on earth you will have many trials and sorrows. But take heart, because I have overcome the world.
~John 16:33, NLT

The Lord Fights FOR You

If God is for us, who can ever be against us?
~ Romans 8:31b, NLT

Remember the original <u>Karate Kid</u>? Those mean dudes in the skeleton unitards are good representations of how the enemy can attack us with negative thoughts, distrust of God, greed, pride, despair, and so on.

When they threaten to beat on us like a pack of bloodthirsty wolves, we can call on and trust in Jesus, our own personal spiritual Mr. Miyagi to whoop up the enemies trying to bully and bruise us.

Though they pack a mean punch and strike with the intent to harm and disable, remember that your attackers hide in fearsome costumes to seem even more threatening than they are. It's nothing but an ugly unitard. In reality, they have already lost. They just haven't given up yet.

Jesus is an undefeated spiritual Ninja Master. We can live undefeated too when we stay tight with Him and trust Him to fight our battles for us.

Empowered: *He fights through you because your weakness displays His strength.*

> *Each time he said, "My grace is all you need. My power works best in weakness." So now I am glad to boast about my weaknesses, so that the power of Christ can work through me.*
> *~ 2 Corinthians 12:9, NLT*

As long as we attempt to maintain our pretense of self-sufficiency, we cut ourselves off from His limitless power. Our inadequacy is the door to His sufficiency. Our weakness opens us to the storehouse of His strength.

> Our inadequacy is the door to His sufficiency. Our weakness opens us to the storehouse of His strength.

Being beat and broken is therefore a gift, because it is then we are willing to turn to God with humble hearts and open arms to receive His strength He's yearning to share with us.

> *The God of peace will soon crush Satan under **your** feet.*
> *~ Romans 16:20, NIV (emphasis mine)*

Since our God is infinitely capable, we need not be concerned by our inadequacies, shortfalls, and deficiencies. He will take whatever we willingly give and use it to achieve victory in our circumstances.

When God asked a timid and faltering Moses to leave his wilderness refuge and courageously demand freedom for His people from a wicked tyrant, He emboldened Moses with a strange question. Moses was arguing with God and highlighting his shortcomings (excuses) for not answering the call. Undeterred, God answered, "Hey, Moe. What are you holding right now? I'll just use that. You don't need anything else because I AM everything." (Exodus 4:2)

God used the very staff Moses was holding to perform wonders never heard or seen before. It was through that very staff that God's power flowed to part the Red Sea.

What if Moses had been holding a rock when God called him? Would it have mattered? Was the important part the staff or the God who operated behind it? God could just as easily use a rock as a stick.

The Lord Fights THROUGH You

It doesn't matter what we have or don't have. It only matters that we submit whatever we've got to God's plan. Then we can just watch Him work through the amazing and the miraculous through our meager offerings.

- Young David, the shepherd, had a **slingshot**. He took down the giant that the entire army feared to approach. (1 Samuel 17)

- A besieged woman had a **millstone**, basically a kitchen appliance. She dropped it on wicked Abimelech's head and saved all the people in her city (Judges 9). (Can you imagine rescuing your whole town by throwing a toaster at the bad guy?)

- A destitute widow had only a small jar of olive **oil**. God multiplied it. She sold it and saved herself and her son (2 Kings 4:1-7).

- Samson had a **donkey's jawbone**. He slew a thousand Philistines and led Israel for 20 years (Judges 15). (Apparently, the Philistines had been trained by Stormtroopers.)

- A young boy had a **sack lunch**. He surrendered it to Jesus, and it fed 5,000 families (John 6).

Through the power of God's spirit, fishermen became apostles, plough-men became judges and generals, ordinary women became conquerors, a shepherd boy became a war hero and beloved King, a carpenter became a Savior, and a dying thief became a saint.

It does not matter to God what we have in our hand. What matters to Him is whether or not our hearts are in His hand. Are we willing to let Him use us? Will we give all we've got, no matter how little it is? Will we have child-like faith to offer our lunch to Jesus while we stare at 15-20,000 hungry people and trust that He will provide abundantly?

Is Your Wood Wet?

If reading about God's love and power didn't get you at least a little pumped up, you need to go back and reread this chapter and give a little more thought to His greatness and His goodness. Jesus, the very Creator of all, gave His all for you because He loves you and doesn't want you to ever be defeated, or even feel like you are. Now, if that don't light your fire, your wood's wet!

So what do we do with a God so good and so great? We kneel in humble gratitude and adoration, and submit all we have and all we are to Him. We turn and surrender to the Love we cannot outrun and receive the powerful protection and supernatural strength of our Maker. We trust Him with our all. And what a sweet surrender it is!

CHAPTER 8

THE SWEET SURRENDER: KNOW WHEN TO GIVE IN

Depending on Your Unchanging God

"Let God have your life; He can do more with it than you can."
~ Dwight L. Moody

Chain of Command

In the military, there is always a clear and precise chain of command. It is absolutely clear who will make the decisions and give the orders, and who will carry out those orders immediately and unflinchingly.

When your job is dealing with life-and-death issues, there's no time for discussion or democracy. The leader calls the shots, and the others obey whether they agree or not. It doesn't matter if the troops are exhausted or hungry or injured, they are expected to follow orders until they are relieved of duty.

Can you imagine the chaos if every soldier did as they thought best without any coordination or consideration of an overall plan? Each fighting unit is a part of the whole. They must all work together in a coordinated effort to be effective against the foe.

The higher up the chain of command you go, the broader the picture with which the decision maker is working. Sometimes things don't make sense on the smaller scale because the bigger picture is obscured from the one in the fight. That's why following the orders of the one who has a bigger picture than you is imperative to victory.

Roger, Sir, You Have the Aircraft

Between our first and second years at the Air Force Academy, we had the choice between two summer programs. We had three weeks of leave, three weeks of SERE (survival training), and three weeks of aerial adrenaline rush. Cadets could either learn how to throw themselves out of a perfectly good aircraft (jump school) or fly and land a plane without an engine (soaring).

After enduring survival training, neither of these two options seemed so intimidating. I chose soaring. The scariest part was that both activities took place on the same field. There was some lateral deconfliction, but we could easily watch our classmates across the field fall out of the sky while we descended at a somewhat slower and only slightly more controlled pace.

I struggled with learning to fly at first. My Instructor Pilot (IP) would fly the glider smoothly and effortlessly behind the tow plane as we ascended, all the while downloading copious amounts of information into my brain. Then he would say, "All right, your turn."

I gave the scripted reply, "Roger, sir, I have the aircraft." (It's necessary to be sure who is flying the plane when there are two people with access to the flight controls. You don't want to find yourself in the situation where you both exclaim, "I thought you had it!" "No, I thought you did! ...")

By the time I controlled the plane for about two seconds, our flight path had become increasingly erratic. We went from flying smooth and level to violently yanking the tow plane all over the sky. I no sooner touched the stick when I heard an almost-but-not-quite panicked voice behind me say a little too forcefully, "I have the aircraft!" (Translation, "Give me control of this thing before you kill us all!")

I acknowledged his command and transfer of control with the standard reply, "Roger, sir, you have the aircraft" as I dropped my hands shamefully into my lap.

Finally, after risking the lives of my IP and tow plane pilot numerous times, it finally clicked. I figured out how to use the rudder pedals. I had been trying to fly the plane like it was a video game by using the stick alone. It turns out, the rudder pedals were put there for a reason, and they come in quite handy when you're trying to fly straight and level behind a tow plane.

The need for my IP to interject and take command lessened as I became more proficient at flying. Eventually, I successfully soloed and earned my wings, but that's another story!

We need to realize that we aren't as awesome at flying through life as we think we are. We would soar so much smoother if we woke each morning and said to God, "Roger, Sir, you have the aircraft." When we continue to act like we know the answers and have the talent when we don't is not only foolish, it's dangerous.

When I flew before I knew what I was doing, it was a risky endeavor for us all. How many people are you going to take down with you before you catch a clue and surrender to the Best Pilot out there? Trust Him to get you where you need to be whether you understand how He's going to do it or not.

Our Place of Submission

Too often, we forget our place. Not only do we forget that we are victorious over the enemy and don't have to let him beat us up, but we also tend to forget that God is God and we are not.

We are the clay. He is our Maker. He has power, authority, and right to do with us as He wills, as much as we have the right to do as we please with the mug we made in pottery class.

Imagine if you got in your car to go to work one morning, and it said to you, "I'm tired of driving you to work. I want to be a dishwasher now." Ludicrous! (Yet, how often do we say essentially the same thing to our Maker?)

You'd tell your car, "A, you weren't built for that; and B, the sole reason I bought you is to drive me where I need to go. That's your purpose—your whole reason for existing in the first place!"

I love how The Message translation puts it:

> *You have everything backward! You treat the potter as a lump of clay.*
> *Does a book say to its author, "He didn't write a word of me"?*
> *Does a meal say to the woman who cooked it, "She had nothing to do with this"?*
> *~ Isaiah 29:16, MSG*

Yes, too often, we get it backward. We are not God. He does not need to answer to us. We are to answer to Him (Romans 9:20).

Without God, what are we anyway? We are nothing more than a glove without a hand or a boot without a foot. He is the power and purpose and direction behind all that we do (Isaiah 10:15).

We can't have Jesus on our terms. He's not ours to control or to censure. He cannot and will not be manipulated by us. Let us not forget who the clay is and Who is the Potter. Too often, we try to mold God into the image we prefer rather than receive Him as He reveals Himself to us.

He is unchanging—the same yesterday, today, and forever. We are fickle and feckless. We need to be the moldable ones rather than constantly trying to stuff and hold Him in a box of our own design. God will never fit nor stay. He is a box-busting God who will not conform to what you wish Him to be—so stop trying.

Me, Submit? Are You Serious?

In our modern culture today, particularly in America, we don't like to be told to submit. Even the word "submit" itself is practically a dirty word. True, some have grossly abused it, but we must remember to Whom we are called to submit. There is no one who loves us more or has sacrificed more for us. He is the One to whom we must surrender if we want to live victoriously.

It is not a chore or burden to place ourselves under the care of One who leads so sacrificially. We are foolish not to subordinate ourselves to the God-man who washes our dirty feet and cleanses our souls from the pollution of sin. The smartest response to One such as this is to eagerly and wholeheartedly default our desires to His plan.

As our Maker, He alone has every right to every part of us. As our Redeemer, He has purchased us with His own life. How can we not offer all that we are and all that we have to Him in response?

Surrender to God

It sounds like an oxymoron, but it's true. Victory lies in surrender. To whom you surrender makes all the difference. Too often, I swallow the lies of the enemy and resist God's efforts to draw me close. I get it backward.

If even the God-man Jesus surrendered to the Father's will though
it led Him to dark and painful
places, how can we not do likewise?
Jesus loved His Heavenly Father and
treasured our freedom more than He
dreaded the cross He had to bear.

> Victory lies in sur-
> render. To whom you
> surrender makes all the
> difference.

Surrender Your Pain

Can you blame the mechanic that your car is still broken if you never gave him the keys or entrusted your car to his care? It's not his fault your car won't run. It's yours.

Are you justified in whining to the doctor that you are still sick when you never took the medicine he prescribed? Is it your physical therapist's fault that you are still in pain when you only did the exercises he gave you for a couple of days and then quit?

Can you blame God that your life is still broken when you haven't surrendered your pain or your problems to Him nor entrusted your wounds to His care? Don't resist the very One who has the power to help you.

Sometimes our pain continues to harass us because we hang on to it and refuse to surrender it to God. Don't let the hurt fester. Identify it. Surrender it to God. Let Him have it. He will take it. Cast your cares on Him. He cares for you (1 Peter 5:7). He wants to take them from you.

Surrender Your Plans

Lay down your desires, plans, fears, hopes, dreams, expectations, and anxious thoughts. Give them to God to handle. In exchange, receive His Godfidence to move forward wherever He wants you to go.

Ask Him to prune your desires and cut off what shouldn't be there. Allow what He desires to grow and bear much fruit. Call out and cut off whatever is in you that is not of God and let it wither.

Anything in your life that is not from God is not what you want anyway.

> *Whom have I in heaven but you? And earth has*
> *nothing I desire besides you.*
> ~ *Psalm 73:25, NIV*

Surrendering means letting go of what we are trying to grab, to embrace all He longs to give. He has so much more for us than the things after which we chase. We are like young children fascinated by the wrapping paper when He's trying to show us the greater gift inside the box.

We must learn the art of becoming a living sacrifice by releasing our death grip on what we want and reach out for what we need to live out the purpose for which we are here.

Surrender Completely

We do not surrender to God because He has overwhelmed us with His power and broken our will to resist. We choose to surrender because He has overcome us by His love, tenderly embracing our weary heart.

Total surrender means we hold nothing back. There is no part of our lives where we say, "Anything but this, Jesus." How can we call Him Lord and still withhold any part of ourselves or our lives from His scrutiny and direction? It can't be done.

It is utterly impossible to serve two masters. We can't have one foot in God's Kingdom and the other in the devil's domain. We must choose. We must be all in one or the other.

Jesus' words have made it clear that He has left no room for fence-sitters. Lukewarm followers are spat out (Revelation 3:16). The only way to live for God is to let our self-centered ways and desires wither and die.

Only by yielding our allegiance to Jesus can we ever hope to achieve victory in this life and the next. He is The Way, The Truth, and The Life (John 14:6). Nobody gets where they need to go without Him. You can't get on the road to triumph by going your own way. Paradoxically, victory lies in surrender.

Die to Yourself, Not to Your Enemy

Endure suffering along with me, as a good soldier of Christ Jesus.
~ 2 Timothy 2:3, NLT

Every soldier must be prepared to give his life for the sake of the cause for which he fights, but he is never expected to lay himself down and die before his enemy willingly.

We are called to be "living sacrifices," meaning dead to our self—our desires, wishes, and plans that are not of God—but living for Christ and used for His glory.

I tell you the truth, unless a kernel of wheat is planted in the soil and
dies, it remains alone. But its death will produce many new ker-
nels—a plentiful harvest of new lives. Those who love their life in
this world will lose it. Those who care nothing for their life
in this world will keep it for eternity.
~ John 12:24-25, NLT

Dying to our self means laying down our desires and plans in exchange for His, trusting that His are better even if they make us feel worse in the short term. I often ask God to make my desires match His, but from time to time, I find that I still have lingering desires of self that are not God's will for me (or at least, not yet).

By allowing our desire to remain even though it does not mirror His own, He gives us the opportunity to deny ourselves and take up our cross, thus joining Jesus in His suffering and, ultimately, His glory. We must be willing to say, "This may not be what I wanted, but I'll receive it with gratitude."

He asks us to take up our crosses daily, with boldness and determination, and without complaining (Philippians 2:14-16). To follow Christ, we must release our own will and embrace His. Like the monkey bars on the playground of our childhood, we must move forward by letting go, so we have a free hand to hold onto what lies ahead.

Looking to Job again, we hear him say, "Shall we accept good from God and not trouble?" (Job 2:10) The Lord gives and takes away (Job 1:21), and we must be willing to accept both to stay in step with our Commander.

His grace is sufficient. You *can* (by His power and grace) bear the cross He's given you even though there will be plenty of days when you are sure you can't take another step. He would not frustrate you by telling you to do the impossible. That's His job. He does the impossible. We just have to follow in obedience, trusting Him to go before us, smoothing our path even as He directs us to the next step (Isaiah 45:2).

Always leading by example, Jesus showed us how to do this. When tempted by the devil, He chose to go hungry rather than to disobey. He rejected shortcuts and "easy" fixes, and depended on God's timing to be perfect. We do well to do likewise saying, "Your will. Your way. Your timing."

For even Christ didn't live to please himself.
~ Romans 15:3a, NLT

Humility

"Many preserve themselves by humbling themselves.
The bullet flies over him who stoops."
~ Matthew Henry

If submission requires surrender, surrender requires humility. It is our pride and arrogance that most often hold us back from surrendering to God.

Fear also prevents us from full surrender. We fear what God will ask of us if we give Him full control. Our fears are often rooted in pride. We fear failure, ridicule, and embarrassment. Our fear of people's opinions propels us to please people rather than God. We fear being inadequate and imperfect in living out what God has called us to do.

It takes humility for us to admit our dependence on God and our inability to know or do the right thing without His guidance and power. We like to pretend that we have it all together, know all the answers, and possess the resources and talent to make it happen.

But isn't this the very same pride that led to Lucifer's downturn in the first place?

God never intended for us to have all the answers, because He hasn't revealed them all. He didn't give us all we need because He wants us to come to Him and know Him as our daily Provider.

The Freedom of Following

I once had the pleasure of accompanying my husband on a business trip to Singapore. This trip was part of building teamwork and camaraderie between our nations as strategic partners to enhance our militaries' abilities to work together.

The hosts of our trip were enthusiastic about showing us all the beauty and wonders of Singapore, and making sure we had the best time possible. For ten days, they treated us to a jam-packed tour of all the 277.6 square-mile island of Singapore had to offer. We went to shows, historical sites, museums, and tried a myriad of various styles of food available in the country.

Every minute of our time was carefully scheduled to maximize our experience of their country. There was no time for jet-lagging! It wasn't on the schedule!

My husband and I had a delightful time. We were free to relax and enjoy the adventure. Our only job was to show up and follow the plan of our hosts. We didn't have to worry about schedules or directions. It had all been laid out in advance.

It was one of our best trips because the planning wasn't our responsibility. The stressful part of travel was a burden we didn't have to bear. We had zero "heated discussions" over maps, or what to see and what to skip. We just enjoyed each other's company and soaked up all the adventure and excitement of our journey.

We never worried about the near future. We weren't given an itinerary in advance. We had no idea what was coming up next, but we knew it would be good. We might have to endure 100% humidity, walk a great distance (despite the protests of my then 6-month pregnant body), or eat something strange, but we knew that at the end of the day, we'd be glad we followed our hosts. And we were! We did not regret a single activity we did.

Wouldn't it be fun to view all of life this way? God has wonderful plans for us! We don't know all the details, but we don't need to. If we'd just relax and let Him be God, we'd probably enjoy the journey a lot more. Too often, we are so busy peppering our Life Coordinator with questions about what's coming up next that we are unable to enjoy the beauty of what He's showing us right now on the way.

Following is not a bad thing or a lesser thing. There is freedom in following if you trust the One you follow and relax in His leadership, trusting Him to manage your life with care and skill.

True freedom is not the autonomy to do whatever you wish. That type of "freedom" is destructive and leads only to anarchy and personal misery. Paradoxically, we find real freedom in submission to Christ. Joyful surrender produces peace when we put all that concerns us into His care and leave it there.

Seek His Protection

I will call upon the Lord, who is worthy to be praised;
so shall I be saved from my enemies.
~ Psalm 18:3, NKJV

In battle, it is foolish to leave yourself undefended and open to attack. Likewise, since we know there is a spiritual enemy stalking us, we must seek cover.

God wants to protect us. He stands ever ready to defend us. The first step is admitting our inability to save ourselves. As long as we try to keep God at arms' length and say, "That's okay, God. I got this," we will never experience true victory because we will always be exposed and vulnerable.

The opening chapters of Job give insight into some of God's protection. With regard to Job's faithfulness to God, the devil complains that God has put a wall of protection around not only Job but his entire household and everything he owned. Job was fruitful, healthy, and prosperous in everything he did.

The devil was grouchy about his inability to mess with Job and anything or anyone in his care. He was only able to enter Job's life and wreak havoc when God agreed to remove the barrier temporarily.

I don't claim to know how all that works in the spiritual realms, but I'm smart enough to say, "Hey, God. I'd like some of that protection of Yours that Job had, please." We must remember, however, that God is God and He gets the final say about what will or won't touch our lives.

We can see from Job's example that following God with all we've got and seeking His protection is not a guarantee of physical or psychological safety. It doesn't work that way. On the contrary, God has promised us that we *will* experience hardship, and that He will always be with us even when He chooses to remove some of His divine protection for a time.

The enemy's got his radar out, seeking another hapless victim. I often ask God to cloak me from the enemy's radar so I can "go stealth" and continue to carry out my God-given mission unhindered. This is the modern military version of "hide me in the shadow of your wings" (Psalm 17:8b) that we looked at in the previous chapter.

There are numerous powerful scriptures about God being our shelter, our fortress, our stronghold, and our shield. Many of these were penned by David who was both a military man and a poet. These verses are excellent fodder for prayer. You can't go wrong speaking God's own words back to Him!

Trust God

Those who know your name trust in you, for you, Lord, have never forsaken those who seek you.
~ Psalm 9:10, NIV

I have vivid childhood memories of me trembling on the edge of the diving board overlooking the ominous deep end. My dad faithfully treaded water, coaxing me to jump in, and waited patiently for me to gather the bravery to do so. I always enjoyed the thrill when I finally jumped in, but every time it took me a while to work up the courage.

Jumping into water way over my head would not have been possible at all if I did not trust my daddy with my life. If I had any question that he might fail to catch me or that he would cruelly hold me under water, I would have never considered standing on the diving board, much less jumping off into the 9-foot abyss of chlorinated water below. I had complete trust in both his love for me and his ability to keep me from drowning.

> *"His glory is invisible, we know not the way he takes, even when he is coming towards us in ways of mercy; but, when his intentions are secret, they are kind."*
> *~ Matthew Henry*

You can't completely surrender to someone you don't trust. Trusting God is necessary to fully surrender to Him and His will for your life. You must trust both His power and His goodness to surrender to whatever He asks of you.

Trusting the Victor is necessary to experiencing victory. Much of our angst is because we simply don't trust God to get it right. We foolishly think we could do better. If only He would listen to our plans. We could help Him out!

This is the real issue, isn't it? Faith comes down to trust. The strength of our faith is determined by the degree to which we trust God and take Him at His word in the absence of evidence.

Trust His Love

> *No, despite all these things, overwhelming victory is ours through Christ, who loved us. And I am convinced that nothing can ever separate us from God's love. Neither death nor life, neither angels nor demons, neither our fears for today nor our worries about tomorrow—not even the powers of hell can separate us from God's love. No power in the sky above or in the earth below—indeed, nothing in all creation will ever be able to separate us from the love of God that is revealed in Christ Jesus our Lord.*
> *~ Romans 8:37–39, NLT*

God is like an all-powerful, all-loving heart surgeon. He is not a cruel or capricious ax murderer. If you're in pain, remember He only makes cuts that lead to healing. God only inflicts the kind of pain that would be cruel to leave undone.

Imagine what would happen if you were awake during your open-heart surgery trying to instruct the surgeon on what to do and how it should be done. Ridiculous! Yet, we do this very thing to God all the time.

> God only inflicts the kind of pain that would be cruel to leave undone.

We trust flawed human beings to operate on our bodies. We rest in a chemically-induced state of sleep while they cut open our bodies and rearrange our organs or pin our bones together. They have earned our trust through their degrees and experience.

How much more do we ought to trust a flawless and all-knowing God? He didn't just study about our bodies in school; He **created** them, and every other part of us as well! Sadly, many of us trust our human doctors more than we trust our Great Physician.

Trust His Heart

God is too wise to be mistaken
God is too good to be unkind
So when you don't understand
When you don't know His plan
When you can't trace His hand trust his heart
~ Babbie Mason

His will is what we would choose if we could understand everything He knows, but since those truths are obscured from us, we must trust the Master's heart toward us.

Resist the temptation to interpret His love based on your experience. "If He loved me, He would have _____." Healed my child, restored my marriage, answered my prayer, etc.

Instead, filter your experience through the lens of His certain and steadfast love for you.

There are many questions and much we don't understand, things we will never know. But we don't need to know more knowledge; we need to know God more. By learning about Him and experiencing His presence, we can trust Him at deeper levels. When life doesn't make sense, trust His heart.

He loves us beyond measure, and there is nothing on earth or in heaven or from hell that can keep us from His love.

Trust His Constancy

Jesus Christ is the same yesterday and today and forever.
~ Hebrews 13:8, NIV

I've never been a fashionista. I don't dress to impress. I dress to be comfortable. I am usually unaware of what is or is not in fashion at any given time. There are a few clothes still in my closet that I had when I got married over 20 years ago.

On the rare occasion that I shop for clothing, I am notorious for undressing mannequins. I can't put an outfit together on my own, but I can point to a statue and say, "I like what she's wearing. Can I have that? I'll take the necklace too."

So that is how it came to be that one day, while watching an animated movie with my children, I heard the fateful comment from one of the characters, "Nobody wears scrunchies anymore."

"Ridiculous!" I thought. "What do you mean 'Nobody wears scrunchies anymore'? I do! All the time!" So I started to intentionally notice how ladies were wearing their hair. After a week of such field research, I reluctantly concluded that nobody wears scrunchies anymore...that is, nobody but me. Somehow, I'd missed that memo.

Embarrassed that I had to learn fashion tips from a cartoon character, I sadly pared down my sizable scrunchie collection to a handful of favorites I could not part with, and donated the rest. (Thrift stores sell antiques, right?) I switched to a plain hair-colored band and lamented the passing of the scrunchie. They were so comfortable! They never pulled my hair or left me with a hair-tension headache at the end of the day.

Life is messy and unpredictable. Just when I get something figured out, it changes. As a military spouse, I laugh at the concept of 5- and 10-year goals. I don't even have a clue where I'll be living this time next year, much less in five years!

Rules change. People's expectations change. Meetings change (and I miss the memo).

God is unchanging (James 1:7, Malachi 3:6). He can't be bribed, convinced, or pressured. He is steady and reliable. When all of life is variable and uncertain, He is the one constant we can always depend on.

He doesn't require one thing of us, and then switch the rules on us mid-game. He never needs to change His mind because He always makes the perfect decision the first time around. He's not angry and vindictive one moment and a roly-poly cosmic pushover the next. He's the same yesterday, today, and forever.

He loved you before you were born, He loves you now, and He'll keep loving you no matter how unlovable you act. He's not fickle. He's not a fair-weather friend. He sticks closer than a brother in every trench, foxhole, or mess you find yourself in or create.

Trust His Faithfulness

Because of the Lord's great love we are not consumed,
for his compassions never fail.
They are new every morning; great is your faithfulness.
~ Lamentations 3:22-23, NIV

I had a plan for exactly how I wanted my family to be. I knew I wanted four children: two boys and two girls. We had a boy first and then a girl. (So far, so good.)

Our daughter was born with a cleft palate, and I had learned that in many countries children with even minor congenital disabilities are thrown away to die unloved and forgotten. This tragic truth stirred in me a desire to adopt a child who might otherwise never experience a loving family and home. But before we could initiate the adoption process, I became pregnant with our third child.

We found out he was a boy, and so I had my two boys and one of my girls. During my pregnancy, I decided that the only way to ensure my fourth child was the girl I desired was to go forward with our plans to adopt and request a girl.

My plan was firmly fixed in my mind when the delivery of my son was an especially long, drawn-out, and painful ordeal. "Yep. No way I'm ever doing *that* again!" I told myself. "Adoption is the way to go!" I told myself.

I'll never forget the moment God changed my mind by touching my heart. As I held my treasured newborn son and marveled at the masterpiece God had created through me, I was overcome with emotion and thought, "How could I *ever* say I don't want to be a part of this astounding miracle again?" I knew then I wanted to have another baby.

Over the next several months, God gradually and gently persuaded me to relinquish my right to craft my family the way I desired and surrender my plan to His. I wanted to trust God, but I was scared. I had so many doubts and questions. How can I do this? What will people think? What if I fail miserably and cause others to think poorly of Christ?

But I had this image in my mind I couldn't escape, of Jesus holding out His hand to me and gently asking, "Do you trust me?"

Oh, Lord. How could I say no? Considering who You are and all You have done for me, how could I answer anything but, "Yes, Lord"? I can't even put the words "no" and "Lord" together. They are utterly incompatible.

Still, reason and my obvious inadequacies tried to convince me to say "No, I can't do what You have asked. It is too hard." But my heart longed to follow Jesus on a wild and uncertain adventure.

Looking back now, I'm so glad I said, "Yes" when I felt God stirring me to trust Him to plan my family, albeit very hesitantly. I had no idea how this adventure would turn out.

I was terrified by my limitations. I was bound by the expectations of my culture. But I just couldn't bring myself to say "No" to One who gave up His glory to die a cruel death as a poor criminal for me.

I won't lie. It's not easy to raise eight children. It's inconvenient to be perpetually pregnant or nursing (or both!) for fourteen years straight. It's discouraging to have so many people call you crazy...to your face...in church no less. It's hard to defy your own culture and do the unexpected. It's difficult to answer the same questions over and over again.

But, oh! What I would have missed out on if I had said no so many years ago. I'm struggling to even come up with the words to describe to you how amazing it is to live with all these young people who just bless my socks off (and drive me bananas sometimes too).

They aren't just children. These little bodies hold the immeasurable treasure of eternal souls within them. Very literally, Heaven and Earth are changed because they exist. I am changed because they exist.

If my family had grown according to my plan, most of my children would not exist. That's very sobering. It makes me wonder what other adventures I may have missed out on because I was too timid to follow Jesus wherever He invited me.

God has been so faithful to us every step of the way. We haven't gotten everything we wanted, but we always have all that we need in Him.

I'm so thankful God's ways are higher and His plans are better. I'm so thankful I said yes! I wouldn't trade it for anything. If I had to do it all over again, I would still say yes. I would just worry less and enjoy it more.

Trust His Timing

He has made everything beautiful in its time. He has also set eternity
in the human heart; yet no one can fathom what God
has done from beginning to end.
~ Ecclesiastes 3:11, NIV

God is always right on time. He is never late or early, but He doesn't cater to our schedule nor coddle our impatience. He teaches us to trust Him even though we see no evidence of new growth or fruitfulness.

When my husband and I were married, we were both on active duty. I was stationed in Texas and he was in New Jersey. We spent our entire engagement and the first six months of our marriage living almost 1,800 miles apart. We were unable to be together, but it was not for lack of trying.

I planned, schemed, plotted, and even begged trying to secure an assignment at the same base as my husband. My frustration mounted as no obstacle even so much as budged no matter how hard I pushed on it or how often I prayed. Why was God doing this? We felt His lead in getting us married, and now it seemed as though we were sentenced to live apart forever.

It took an entire year, but finally, a new job opened up. I applied for the position and got it. Though the base I was trying to get to was overmanned, a higher level created a brand-new position. We newlyweds could finally live together! We were elated!

As I was settling in my new job, I had to clean out the safe where they kept all the classified documents. During this process, I stumbled upon a stack of paperwork. It was a conversation consisting of letters, emails, and memos that preserved a record of how this brand-new position I was in came to be.

I dug into the past through the paper trail and discovered something that made me stop in my tracks—the date on the very first piece of paper. It turns out, the work to create the new position I was now holding had started a year earlier. This was around the time my husband and I got engaged and started praying for an assignment together.

I was holding concrete evidence that God had been working on our behalf for the past year. While I was discouraged at the lack of progress my efforts and prayers seemed to make, God was silently and imperceptibly working in the background the whole time.

Nine states away in a small office I didn't know existed, He was laying the groundwork to create an entirely new position that had never existed before. I was in awe at His perfect provision and flawless timing.

Habakkuk 3:17-19 was a precious verse to me at that time in my life.

Even though the fig trees have no blossoms, and there are no grapes on the vines; even though the olive crop fails, and the fields lie empty and barren; even though the flocks die in the fields, and the cattle barns are empty, yet I will rejoice in the LORD! I will be joyful in the God of my salvation! The Sovereign LORD is my strength! He makes me as surefooted as a deer, able to tread upon the heights.
~ Habakkuk 3:17-19, NLT

Be patient with God's pace. He knows just the right time for everything and how long it must take. God is more focused on quality than speed. He wants what's best for us, and that's not always what is fastest. The infinite, eternal God is patient and thorough, never rushed or hurried. Believe me, He has **all** the time He needs!

God loves you too much to serve you a half-baked cake. Give Him time to cook His plan completely before He reveals it to you. (2 Corinthians 1:20, 2 Peter 3:8, Acts 1:7, Ecclesiastes 3:11) God has a good reason for the apparent delay, even if He never reveals the reason to you.

> God is more focused on quality than speed. He wants what's best for us, and that's not always what is fastest.

We only see the messy middle. We must refrain from judging God's work before its time has come. He has made everything beautiful "in its time" (Ecclesiates 3:11).

God is eternal and exists outside of time. From His perspective, all is complete, and He has already rested from all His work. It is finished. We are souls meant for eternity, and yet we are trapped on a planet spinning relentlessly through time, one day at a time. We cannot comprehend His reckoning of time.

Time is not linear for Him. He can see the whole picture all at once. We are like ants in a line marching along one miniscule section of His grand masterpiece. We are too close and too small to grasp His Big Picture. Therefore, we must trust His timing.

The Sweet Surrender

It is impossible for us to calculate the total impact of our surrender to God's will, not just for those who share our world now, but for future generations as well. Only God Himself knows the full ramifications of our trust in Him.

Ask yourself right now, "What do I need to surrender to you, Lord?" Listen quietly and be open to considering what He brings to mind. Make a list of areas you want to release to God. Mark across it in red pen, "Surrendered to the will of God."

Now that we are better acquainted with our enemy and know the love and power of our God, it is imperative we learn who we truly are. If we don't think about ourselves the same thoughts God thinks of us, we will continue to stumble through life as victors who feel like losers. You are the Beloved of God. Read on to learn how God sees you.

CHAPTER 9

BELOVED: KNOW YOUR WORTH

Receiving God's Unwavering Love

*"The God who beckons you to love more and more cannot love you
more. No matter how you grow in diligence and obedience, you cannot
increase His affection for you. No matter how faithful you become,
you won't get a boost in your lovability. At your darkest moment, you
were loved to the fullest measure; the same is true
at your lightest moment."*
~ Beth Moore

In God's Eyes

I am a dork. I used to say this often when I'd mess up. But I realized
that when I speak of myself this way in front of my children, I am
modeling self-condemnation to these young hearts who are watching
me. I am teaching them by my example the exact opposite of the
beautiful Psalm 139:14.

*I praise you, for I am fearfully and wonderfully made. Wonderful are
your works; my soul knows it very well.*

When we put ourselves down, we are criticizing God's handiwork in us. He has made us for Himself, and He thinks we are
beautiful just the way we are. Who are we to disagree?
I love Zephaniah 3:17.

The LORD your God is with you, the Mighty Warrior who saves. He will take great delight in you; in his love he will no longer rebuke you, but will rejoice over you with singing.

Can you hear it? Can you hear the Lord rejoicing over you with singing? If there's a message in your head telling you that you are a miserable failure who is unwanted, rejected, abandoned, and unworthy of love, you can be sure that is not God's voice you hear because that is not His song.

If you paid attention in Chapter 6, you should be able to recognize that now as the voice of the enemy. Tell that lie to get lost and listen again for God's love song washing over you.

It's there. I promise. You may not have been aware of it, or perhaps the noise and chaos of life have drowned it out, or you heard it but you refused to believe it, but it's there, and it's true.

God rejoices over you—just you! Not your accomplishments, achievements, awards or good deeds. You are enough for Him to delight in just the way you are with all your beautiful imperfections and messy humanness.

He adores you because He fashioned you Himself with great care and compassion. He has molded you for a specific purpose, and you honor Him when you live out that purpose with joy and gratitude.

God has a more expansive perspective than we can comprehend. We see ourselves as we are and what we've done. He looks right past all that nonsense to the essence of our core. He sees who we will become when we surrender to His grace and power. We see our failures, faults, and shortcomings. He sees our future selves perfected by the victory of His sinless Son.

Instead of calling myself a dork, I ought to say, "I am a delight to my Creator, and I can't always hear it, but I know He is rejoicing over me with singing right now." Because *that's* the truth.

What if instead of putting ourselves down, we claimed our worth as God's beloved masterpiece? How could that simple belief transform the way we interact with every person we know?

When we are unplugged from our insecurities and grounded in God's affection for us, we are free to love others recklessly and give our whole selves to them unselfishly. What amazing things would

God accomplish through us for His Eternal Kingdom if we lived like that?

To Whose Voice Are You Listening?

It is our enemy, not God, who tells us we are unlovable, unwanted, and unworthy.

> When we are unplugged from our insecurities and grounded in God's affection for us, we are free to love others recklessly and give our whole selves to them unselfishly.

A scene from the 1989 Steven Spielberg movie *Always* portrays my mental picture of how the enemy messes with us in our heads. The story is about an experienced and daring pilot, Pete (Richard Dreyfuss) who was killed in a crash and subsequently became an angel-like unseen mentor to an up-and-coming younger pilot, Ted (Brad Johnson).

At first, Pete resented his new job and didn't take it seriously. In one scene, Ted was checking himself out in the mirror, and Pete mockingly told him, "You look stupid." At which point, Ted's face fell, revealing that he heard the remark at some deep inaudible level, and not only that but more tragically, he believed it. He accepted the unkind remark without questioning it, and it then became a part of how he saw himself.

Beloved, we must not accept the lies our enemy whispers to us. We must not allow them to infiltrate our thinking.

The Voice of Truth

When we look in the mirror, we must choose to listen to the Voice of Truth—God's voice—the One who made us in His image for His glory and has loved us since before He breathed us into existence. Learn to know and recognize His voice so you can pick it out from the other voices that call out to you and from all the background noise of our busy lives.

Let your mind be renewed by Christ, not defeated by the devil.

*For he has rescued us from the dominion of darkness and brought us
into the kingdom of the Son he loves, in whom we have redemption,
the forgiveness of sins.*
~ *Colossians 1:13-14, NIV*

Lest you think I'm crazy and throw this book down, I don't mean literal audible voices in your head. I'm using "voices" as a metaphor for messages. Receive messages God sends you through His Word. Pitch any thought or idea that does not align with God's Love Letter to you as written in His Word.

I once had a pastor who often encouraged us to "chew the meat and spit the bone." That's what we need to do with the messages we are bombarded with on a daily basis. Don't continue to gnaw on those old bones the devil has handed you to keep you distracted from all that God has for you and wants you to do and experience.

The devil wants to kill, steal, and destroy God's good plans for you.

Don't. Let. Him!

Stand strong on the firm foundation of God's truth and who He says you are.

When the Israelites stood on the verge of receiving their great land of promise and provision, they turned away in fear and faithlessness. Instead of entering rest and abundant living, they wandered the desolate desert for another 40 years circling the same old mountain. Why?

They failed to claim their promise because they had a warped view of themselves. Those sent to investigate the land to see if what God said about the land was true came back with this report: "We were like grasshoppers in our sight, and so we were in their eyes." (Numbers 13:33)

They saw only their lack, inadequacy, and smallness. Assuming their insufficiency was evident to all who saw them, those who failed to claim the blessings God intended them to have made no declaration of who they were in God's eyes.

What is more important: how you see yourself, how others perceive you (or how you think they do), or who God knows you truly are?

Caleb said they could do it (Numbers 13:30) and Joshua encouraged them that God would give them the land (Numbers 14:8).

They didn't **have** to be strong enough to take it; God would hand it over. The ones who felt strong and eager to obey were the ones who trusted in God and His view of them, ignoring what they thought of themselves or imagined others might think of them.

Could the great God who parted the sea for them not work miraculous things through obedient "grasshoppers"?

Beloved

I am my beloved's and my beloved is mine.
~ Song of Solomon 6:3, NIV

You cannot claim your identity in Christ if you don't know what He says about you. Search the Scriptures to discover who God says you are, claiming that as your truth regardless of what contrary message swirls around you or within you.

There should be no discrepancy between the names God calls us and the names we call ourselves. Read and believe this confession. Read it every day if you struggle to feel God rejoicing over you with singing.

> There should be no discrepancy between the names God calls us and the names we call ourselves.

By God's mighty power and boundless grace, I am:

Redeemed (Galatians 3:13)
Beloved (Romans 8:38-39)
Beautiful (Song of Solomon 4:7)
Unashamed (Psalms 34:5)
Renewed (2 Corinthians 4:16)
Held (Deuteronomy 33:27a)
A new creation (2 Corinthians 5:17)
Forgiven (1 John 1:9)
Flawless (Song of Solomon 4:7)
Overcomer (1 John 4:4)
Uncondemned (Romans 8:1)
Free (John 8:36)

Wonderfully made (Psalms 139:14)
Strong (Daniel 10:19)
Chosen (Ephesians 1:11)
Unafraid (1 Timothy 2:7)
Part of a family (Ephesians 1:5-6)
Eternal (John 3:16)
Perfected (Hebrews 10:14)
Completed (Philippians 1:6)
Equipped (2 Timothy 3:17)
Lavished in grace (Ephesians 1:7-8)
Never forgotten (Isaiah 49:16)
Unaccusable (Romans 8:33-34)
Victorious (Romans 8:31)
Held together by Jesus (Colossians 1:17)
Holy and blameless (Ephesians 1:4)
Righteous (Romans 3:22, 5:17)
God's masterpiece (Ephesians 2:10, ESV)
Priceless, worth any sacrifice (Romans 8:32, 5:8)

Don't be the prince or princess living like a beggar because you failed to accept and embrace your birthright. Live beautiful because you are beautiful. God doesn't make ugly junk. You are a rare and precious treasure. Don't listen to anything that tells you otherwise.

Don't believe what the media or your culture says you should be. Believe what God says you already are.

Learning to Love Yourself

You are altogether beautiful, my love; there is no flaw in you.
~ Song of Solomon 4:7, ESV

Sometimes, we selfishly want what we perceive to see as best for ourselves, but often give less than our best to others. At such times, we must remember to consider others better than ourselves (Philippians 2:3).

However, sometimes we selfishly give others all we've got while we play the martyr and hope for pity. Then we must remember to serve God and others better by properly appreciating and caring for ourselves.

These are two ditches on either side of the road. We may think one looks better than the other, but both miss the mark. Neither error keeps us on the straight and narrow path to victory on God's terms.

Both self-centered narcissism and self-deprecating neglect are rooted in pride. (There's Satan's original failure again! Do you see a trend here?) Both have more to do with ourselves and how we want to be perceived than how we want to love and honor God by serving His people generously and with a good attitude.

If we don't love the people whom God has made in His image, we don't love God. Neither can we say we love God and despise, reject, or neglect one of the masterpieces of His creation—ourselves. We are made in His image. We mustn't spoil His image in us by refusing to love and value ourselves.

God's Greatest Commandment

When asked what God's most important commandment is, Jesus responded that it is to love God with all we've got (Mark 12:28-31). He followed that up immediately with the necessity of loving our neighbor. If we love God, then we will also love people because He loves them (1 John 4:20).

Christians talk about these verses often, but there is part of the verse that we usually overlook. Let's look at what Jesus said.

> *Love the Lord your God with all your heart and with all your soul and with all your mind and with all your strength.' The second is this: 'Love your neighbor as yourself.'*
> *~Mark 12:30, NIV*

Those last two words are the part we skip over too often—"as yourself." If we are going to be able to love our neighbor as ourselves, then it implies we must first love ourselves.

We are called to love ourselves—not in a selfish, worldly, me-first, pride-filled sort of way, but one that includes a deep love for God as well as a compassionate love for people.

Value Yourself Because You Are Valuable to God

God does not want us to hate ourselves, consider ourselves worthless, or beat ourselves up. Self-loathing is not humility. It is an affront to God—labeling what He has lovingly created for His glory as unacceptable, unredeemable, and unlovable.

Putting ourselves down is just another form of pride. Whether we are focused on ourselves in positive or negative ways, we have still shifted our center from God to ourselves.

Yes, we are unworthy of His affection. Yes, we can never be perfect or save ourselves. But we are genuinely acceptable, totally redeemable, and utterly lovable. Why? Because He said so. He loved us first. He looks past our unloveliness and sees all the wonderfulness He created us to be. He longs for us to believe and embrace the truth of who we are.

Learning to Care for Yourself

Sometimes, self-care feels selfish, especially if we're used to neglecting ourselves. But taking care of ourselves is not selfish. It's being a good steward of the body, brain, and time God has entrusted to us.

Just as we must love ourselves emotionally to be able to love others, so we must care for ourselves practically to have the strength to serve others. How can you love others if you don't love yourself enough to even take care of your most basic needs?

We can't pour anything from an empty pitcher. Make a commitment to nurture and nourish yourself.

Five Ways to Start Loving Yourself Better Today

Self-care is important in the same five areas of our personhood we discussed in Chapter 6. Why? Because these are the battlegrounds where our enemy attacks us. We must resist attack by keeping these parts of ourselves strong, healthy, and vibrant. Neglecting ourselves in any area leaves us vulnerable.

Spirit:

- Spend daily personal time with God any way you can for however long you can. Include prayer and Bible reading or study.

- Worship isn't just for Sunday! Turn up your favorite praise music and sing with joyful noise about the goodness and greatness of God.

- Plug into a church community with wholehearted worship, Biblical teaching, and meaningful fellowship. Make regular and consistent church attendance a habit.

- Meditate on God's word often. How can you apply what you learn to your own life?

Mind:

- Allow God to transform the way you think. Don't conform to the world's mold of thought patterns. Renew and refresh your thinking with spiritual truths. Cultivate a Biblical worldview based on God's truth, not your culture's opinion.

- Trust God's plan. Embrace His peace.

- Continually learn, grow, discover, and engage.

- Your brain is like a muscle. Disuse leads to atrophy. Use it or lose it! Learn new things. Figure out puzzles. Play chess.

- Read books and listen to audiobooks. Chew on new ideas and filter them through your Biblical worldview.

- Make a habit of thinking victorious thoughts. If you think like you're defeated, you will be. If you think tough, you'll be tough.

Will:

- Ignite your passion.

- Inspire your motivation.

- Invest your skills, talents, and gifts so you can live out your purpose. (Don't bury your talents!)

- Avoid burnout through self-care and rest.

- Combat discouragement from lack of recognition or appreciation by knowing the value God places on the work you do.

- Commit and do it. Don't keep making the same decisions over and over. Decide once and for all, and go for it.

- Be persistent. Setbacks, obstacles, and failures are part of the game. Don't let them stop you from experiencing the purpose and the pleasure of God.

Emotions:

- Count your blessings, not your burdens.

- Pause to enjoy the simple moments and joys of life deliberately.

- Maintain healthy and meaningful friendships in addition to your family.

- If you're a stay-at-home mom or dad, be deliberate about creating opportunities for conversation with other adults.

- Make date night with your spouse a priority (A DIY date at home after the kids go to bed counts too!)

- Nurture hobbies and engage in activities you do just for the fun of it.

- Hold on to hope and don't let go no matter how dark it gets.

Body:

- Fuel your body with the nourishment in needs.

- Get enough sleep. Make it a priority over your to-do list.

- Drink plenty of water. Proper hydration is a simple way to solve a lot of physical problems.

- Exercise. Find a way that you enjoy moving and do it frequently. It doesn't have to be long or difficult. A daily walk is a great way to move your body and enjoy God's creation.

These topics are discussed in-depth and in much greater detail in Book 2 of the Stand Strong Series, *UNDAUNTED: Your Battle Plan for Victorious Living*. In *UNDAUNTED*, I will guide you through a practical battle plan you can use every day in each of these five critical areas to empower you to live victoriously through Christ's strength.

Let's Get Real: Be Transparent

It is okay to not be okay. If you are not okay, you don't have to pretend that you are okay. You can say, "I need help. I need help from God."
~ based on James 5:16 by Joyce Meyer

Giving your real self (as God created you to be) to the world can be scary because it requires vulnerability and authenticity. These are skills that don't come naturally to a lot of people (myself included!).

How Many Times Can I Fail in One Day?

If I must boast, I would rather boast about
the things that show how weak I am.
~ 2 Corinthians 11:30, NLT

Vulnerability can look messy. Don't believe me? Read on.

One day, I got a call from the school nurse that my daughter was ill. So I made a same-day appointment for her, canceled my afternoon plans, and picked her up from school.

I drove to the doctor with her and my two youngest children, and met my husband at the doctor's office on base to pass the two littles back to him so they could go home and get a nap (my littles, not my husband). Fortunately, he finished work early that afternoon and was able to help me out. A rare treat for a military spouse.

As I was walking in the door to my house, I got a call from the school secretary saying that no one was at the bus stop to meet my kindergartener, so the bus driver was bringing her back to school. *Oh yeah!* Her two older brothers both had after-school activities that day, and I had her older sister. There was no one left to walk her home—a detail I had overlooked in all my rushing to and fro.

I apologized to the secretary and told her I had just walked in the door with my daughter, but I used the wrong girl's name. She corrected me and said I couldn't possibly have my daughter because she was on the bus going back to school! *Oh, never mind! No point in explaining that I really can remember what I named my children, if given enough time.* I grabbed my keys and left again.

I raced to get back in the van and asked my sick daughter to tell her dad that I was leaving again. He called me while I was on my way to ask what was going on. After I explained my failure to my husband, he informed me that he had to go pick up our teen daughter from track practice at a different school. He couldn't leave until I got back because our children who were old enough to babysit the younger ones were all at other activities.

I arrived at the school to find it empty. No secretary. No daughter. No bus. I stood lost for a moment, wondering what to do next, when my phone rang. It was my oldest teen son. He had my kindergartener and was walking her home. *What?! I thought the bus driver was taking her back to the school! I thought you were at work!*

Apparently, the bus driver saw my son walking home from his job and recognized him as the older brother of the forgotten child. So she stopped the bus and handed my daughter over to her big brother. I'm sure the bus driver was eager to find a responsible family member to claim my child. That was why my daughter never arrived back at the school.

So I headed home once again. My teen son and my poor abandoned daughter got home ahead of me. My bewildered husband was trying to piece together why I drove to pick up our daughter from school, but she came home with her brother instead. (*Wasn't he working today?*)

I asked my son how the bus driver knew that he was the older brother of her unclaimed passenger. As a military family, we had only recently moved to the area and didn't know many people on the tiny island where we were living.

It turned out that the bus driver had a second job as my son's supervisor at the local grocery store. (The town we were living in is so small it's called a "village.") She knew his younger siblings because they had come to the store before to see their big brother in action at the checkout register. (*Yeah, he loved our visit about as much as you think he did.*)

There wasn't much time for chit chat though. My husband and I "high-fived," passing command of the household and all therein from him to me, and he raced out the door to go pick up our oldest from high school track practice.

Shortly after he left, I remembered that I was supposed to give someone information to include in a newsletter. *Oh dear! I had missed the deadline!* I quickly fired off my inputs in an email, only to learn later that she had to send the newsletter out without my information because I was too slow in responding.

And all of that is just one afternoon in the life of a mother of eight children. I'm exhausted and anxious all over again just from writing it out!

Par for My Course

If this scenario were just a one-time occurrence, a wild exception, or a fateful fluke, it would be easier for me to deal with it, but sadly, it's not. There are so many times in life I feel like I fail more often than I succeed. Many days are one step forward and two steps back—over and over again.

I hate to confess this wasn't the first time no one was there to pick up our kindergartener. One time the principal even drove her to our house because no one could reach me on the phone. (In my defense, I was on an airplane with my phone obediently switched to airplane mode at that exact moment. But that's a whole different story!) Can you see why homeschooling eight children is in some ways easier than sending them to public school?

The week before this comedy of errors happened, I had just barely missed my daughter's Native American presentation at school due to a miscommunication (they changed the time and didn't tell everyone). She was sobbing by the time I got there, and her sweet teacher allowed us some extra time for a special one-on-one presentation by ourselves.

My daughter was very understanding, and it all ended well, but boy, did I feel like the worst-mom-of-the-year recipient when I first got to the school. All the other on-time parents had stared me down as my daughter's eyes filled with tears! Oh, the shame and humiliation of being *the one* who didn't get the memo.

The weekend after this, our family was two hours late to the AWANA awards (because yours truly wrote down the wrong time in her overbooked planner). We arrived just as everyone else was leaving. The upside was that it didn't matter that I didn't have time to brush the girls' hair after all. No one even saw them.

The downside was the kids missed out on the ice cream party afterward. I'm **so glad** children excel at forgiving the repentant! Making kids miss an ice cream party is a ***huge*** mommy fail of epic proportions. (Don't worry, concerned citizens. We got them a treat elsewhere and we detect no permanent psychological damage or emotional scarring.)

Transparency Is Messy

So that's what transparency can look like. You might be thinking, "Umm. Excuse me, but your flaws are showing. In fact, they are hanging out all over the place! Put that unsightly business away!"

But this is me. This is my real life. It's messy and wonderful, crazy and blessed. Time with my family can be total chaos and utter bliss all at the same time. I don't want my life to be any other way. God knew what He was doing when He brought us all together, and we trust Him to see us through this wild ride.

Every time I try to argue with God and tell Him that I don't have what it takes to raise eight children well, He abruptly reminds me that He already knows. *"Shoot, girl! You don't even have what it takes to bring **one** child up in righteousness, let alone **eight**! That's why I'm here. I already know you're inadequate. I just need you to realize you aren't enough so that you will depend on Me and My all-sufficiency. With Me, nothing is impossible. Let Me do all the heavy lifting. You just learn to relax more and enjoy the thrill of the ride!"*

Why don't I tell this story more often? Why did I wait to tell it publicly...in a book? It comes down to pride.

I don't want you to think I'm a loser mom. I don't want to hear you say that I'm in over my head. I don't want to have to bravely face that condemning look in your eye or to have you exclaim, "What?! You forgot your child *and* called her by the wrong name? That's it! I'm calling CPS on you."

Transparency Destroys Pride

The good thing about transparency is that it destroys our pride. Pride annihilation is a good thing. Remember Lucifer from Chapter 5? Remember what started his downward spiral to hell? Yep. Pride.

When I look at my life, there is no way I can claim credit for all the beauty and grace it holds. I *know* it's not because of me. I'm the lady who forgets her kid at the bus stop! Every wonderful thing in my life is from God alone. He gets all the credit!

And if that means that outsiders see me as a loser mom, then so be it. My God, my husband, and my children all know the depths of love in my heart even when my outward actions are less-than-stellar. They know the Grace by which I stand. They love my imperfectly ridiculous self, even when I accidentally call them by the wrong name or mess up our precariously balanced schedule.

And as I tell my story, my *real* story, I am set free from my prison of performance and run unfettered as I truly am—messy and beloved. And maybe, just maybe, I can embolden you to do the same.

Give the Gift of Your True Self

"Vulnerability is absolutely transformative
and creates more trust, not less."
~ Jen Hatmaker, For the Love

It's risky to be transparent. We humans can sometimes be very hard on each other. Our honest confessions may not be received well. We might leave feeling misunderstood, alone, ignorant, or unspiritual.

Sadly, that happens sometimes—even among those of us who say we are saved by grace.

But I believe the benefits of transparency are worth the risks. I sense a common theme, especially among women today, that we are tired of posts and pins that only show the beautiful and the impeccable and leave out the messier parts of our lives.

We have exhausted ourselves trying to serve dinner like a cooking show, mother like the parenting book says we should, craft like a Pinterest champ, decorate like HGTV, and all the while looking like a Photoshopped model. We have unattainable standards set before us, and we buy into them all too easily. No wonder we feel defeated. I feel a collective, "Enough already!" rising within us.

> We need to listen without criticism, love without judgment, accept without shock, and serve without superiority.

It's time to be brave and get real, and give others permission to do the same. Life is hard enough without us nitpicking at each other. We need to listen without criticism, love without judgment, accept without shock, and serve without superiority. That's what Jesus did, and that's the transparency we all crave. Let us each become the response we are longing to receive from others.

And actually, people are usually not as critical we imagine them to be. More often than not, real honesty produces more "me too's" than "shame on you's." It's what we imagine people might say rather than their actual words that hold us back from sharing openly.

Those who fall into the shame-on-you camp have probably not yet admitted or come to terms with their own shortfalls and are still caught in the trap of trying to cover their inadequacies with false superiority. Focusing on the flaws of others allows them to divert attention from focusing on their own. Many of us do this every day without even realizing it.

Usually, once we do open up, others around us breathe out a sigh of relief that they are not alone. In truth, others will draw their courage to share by witnessing the transformative power of transparency in us. When we share our truth and allow others the same freedom to share theirs, the farce of isolation melts away, and we find a life-giving community.

Transparency with God

Worship and serve him with your whole heart and a willing mind.
For the LORD sees every heart and knows every plan and thought.
If you seek him, you will find him.
~ 1 Chronicles 28:9, NLT

Vulnerability is necessary for a true connection with God and people. When we stay hidden, no one knows who we really are. But before we can get real with real people, we have to learn to be authentic with God. In case you haven't heard, He already sees right through us anyway, even when we pretend He can't.

Would not God find this out? For He knows the secrets of the heart.
~ Psalm 44:21, NASB

You may be wondering why we need to make an effort to be transparent with a God who knows us better than we know ourselves. Getting honest with God will do nothing to add to His knowledge of us, but it will deepen our understanding of ourselves.

God knows what is in us, but He wants us to name it and own it, even if it's messy or ugly. There is nothing we can uncover about ourselves that will cause Him to love us any less. And it is impossible for Him to love us anymore because He already loves us infinitely, just as we are. We are imperfectly beautiful and treasured beyond measure in His sight.

When, in sincerity and repentance, we expose our failures to His Pure Light, He does not scorch us by His holiness. Instead, the light of His Love extinguishes the darkness within us, and our once-cold heart is strangely warmed with His grace-filled acceptance of our true identity.

His Perfect Power in the Middle of Our Mess

We want our lives to bring glory to God, but maybe our ideas about what brings Him glory are skewed. We think we will glorify God when we have our act together. But I think God is trying to tell us something different. Here's what He told Paul.

> *Each time he said, "My grace is all you need. My power works best in weakness." So now I am glad to boast about my weaknesses, so that the power of Christ can work through me. That's why I take pleasure in my weaknesses, and in the insults, hardships, persecutions, and troubles that I suffer for Christ. For when I am weak, then I am strong.*
> *~ 2 Corinthians 12:9-10, NLT*

God's power and grace shine brightest through the cracks of our brokenness. We need to *admit*—Paul even goes so far as to *boast*—in our weakness, for it showcases God's power and strength. Our weakness allows others to see God at work in our lives without our personal strengths blocking their view. That's a transparency God can use to transform lives and soften stiff hearts.

> God's power and grace shine brightest through the cracks of our brokenness.

We yearn to be known and accepted and loved just as we are, not as we should be, right here in the middle of our mess. God loves every one of us like that. And if we drink deeply of His grace, we will love others that way too.

- God sees the beauty in our hearts even when our outward expression of the treasure we hold inside is not Pinworthy.

- God knows how deeply we care for our people even on those days when we lose it, or forget it, or blow it.

- God watches us as we faithfully serve in thousands of ways that no one ever sees and will never be acknowledged.

- God displays the artwork of our lives for His glory even when we color outside the lines or break our crayons.

His heart is for us. And when we grasp that—when we really get it—it becomes easy to have the heart for all people, especially the messy ones, because we know that we all need to be loved like that, especially when it's our turn to be the messy one.

It takes great boldness to disassemble the protective walls we build around ourselves and step forward to allow God to display His power through our weakness. But guess what? No one is ever going to get saved because I had my act together.

It is God who transforms lives, and He loves to display His awesomeness through broken, messy people who may not even be sure what act we're on much less how to get it together. So I guess that includes me! (Don't you want to be included too?)

On the other hand, it doesn't require any courage to pretend like everything's okay. It takes no grit to act like we are responding to everything life is throwing at us with unshakable faith and unwavering hope.

So go ahead. Be courageous. Share your truth. Allow God to shine His grace through the cracks of your brokenness. Use your story to highlight your Savior. Give the gift of your true self. The world needs the real you. It's okay to let our faults show. People should already know we're human, and that humans are imperfect and messy. Maybe the ones who can't admit that yet just need us to show them how.

Let us commit to ready ourselves to listen with the heart of Jesus when someone else is ready to share their story or reveal their weakness. Jesus spoke to many people who were far from having their act even remotely together. As we read the gospels and listen to how these desperate people responded to Him, it is clear that though He brought their weaknesses to light, He was always gentle and kind. May we ever remember His unwavering compassion when a broken person stands before us.

Unbridled Transparency Is Not a Good Idea

Even as we are authentic, we must be discerning when sharing our more personal and tender parts. Being real does not require us to reveal all we've got to everyone. Not everything needs to be shared with everybody. We all need a few folks with whom we can share anything and everything.

But not everybody has earned the right to be trusted with the full content of our story. We must not be too quick to toss our hard-earned pearls before unappreciative swine just for the sake of transparency.

God-honoring transparency means we don't sit in the corner with our parka on and our head down, hiding our light under necessary bundling. It does **not** mean we streak across the stage on our way to skinny dip in the pool of TMI. Please share with discernment, y'all.

We must also be intentional to refrain from uncovering things that ought not to be shared. It never honors Christ for us to speak poorly of others (our spouse, friends, family, pastor, even strangers). Gossip in the name of transparency is still gossip. It is hurtful and goes against God's best for us.

Being transparent requires wisdom, discernment, discretion, and tact, so we are careful not to overshare. In my writing, I make a point to share only my own stories, and not stories that belong to others. We do not have the right to announce another person's journey without explicit permission to do so. It is for them to choose when, how, and with whom they will share their story.

A Beloved Warrior

Let us make an effort to study who God says we are, and then soak it in until we believe it in the deepest parts of our being. By experiencing God's love for us, we will grow to love ourselves, which frees us to be beautifully imperfect and real.

Not only are you God's beloved child, but you were created to be a victorious warrior. In the next chapter, we'll look at the many ways God equips us to walk in victory and push back the darkness that threatens to engulf us.

CHAPTER 10

UNDEFEATED: CLAIM YOUR VICTORY

Embracing Your Undefeated Life

"Our deepest fear is not that we are inadequate. Our deepest fear is that we are powerful beyond measure. It is our light, not our darkness, that most frightens us. Your playing small does not serve the world. There is nothing enlightened about shrinking so that other people won't feel insecure around you. We are all meant to shine as children do. It's not just in some of us; it is in everyone. And as we let our own lights shine, we unconsciously give other people permission to do the same. As we are liberated from our own fear, our presence automatically liberates others."
~ Marianne Williamson

Created to Win

God did not create us to keep us defeated. He intends for us to walk in victory. However, when we do life backwards, submitting to the enemy and resisting God, we feel defeated.

The Ultimate Loser

"Argue for your limitations, and sure enough they're yours."
~ Richard Bach

At the Academy, if you weren't an intercollegiate athlete, you were required to play an intramural sport against the other squadrons. The upperclassmen decided who was on what team. They put themselves on the fun teams like ultimate Frisbee.

My first year, I got stuck on the cross-country running team, not because I was a good runner but because it was a less desirable sport and I was a freshman. I guess the upperclassmen weren't too concerned about our squadron winning intramural sports.

A couple of times a week, I would race against team members from other squadrons. Most people on the cross-country teams were either good runners or unfortunate freshmen. We ran a big loop around the outside of the athletic fields. As we crossed the finish line, we were each handed a Popsicle stick with a number on it. Nearly every race, I got handed a stick bearing the number 1 or 2.

At that point, I had to humbly approach the upperclassmen responsible for keeping score and confess that I was not the first or even the second finisher of the race. I had to explain out loud that I was the *last* runner from the *previous* race, not the top runner from the current heat.

They would then take back my Popsicle stick and exchange it for one that had a number on it somewhere in the teens. I distinctly remember one such occasion when an upperclassman remarked, "Oh! That explains it. I was wondering why we had an extra stick!" So happy I could clear that up for you, Sir.

If that is not the definition of an ultimate loser, I don't know what is. I guess I could've taken a more Biblical approach. Realizing that the last shall be first, I could have just kept the #1 Popsicle stick. But that didn't seem right.

Everyone has had their fair share of loser moments, but that defeated feeling we get when we fail or fall short (or run slow!) is a lie. In actuality, we can all be victors in Jesus.

I don't have to be good enough, smart enough, talented enough, or athletic enough. Jesus has offered to exchange the benefits of His perfect life with the penalties of my messy one. It's not a fair trade, but that's what grace is!

Fight Your Battle with Your Focus on God

Stand firm and you will win life
~ Luke 21:19, NIV

I cannot overemphasize the importance of developing a Christ-centered self-perception based on truth. We must know, claim, and act out of who God says we are—not who the enemy or the world, or even our friends say we are.

When a scrawny teenager ran to the battle line to stand toe to toe against a 9-foot professional soldier, he knew (as did everyone else) that if he fought in his own strength, he was going to get pulverized.

Instead, he yelled, "You may have your ginormous weapons and huge biceps, but I'm on God's side, and you've just really ticked Him off. So look out, buddy. You're going down!" (My paraphrase of 1 Samuel 17:45) Like David, you win because of Who's backing you up when the bully tries to pick on you, not because you work out at the gym six days a week.

Contrast David's attitude with that of the Israelites. When faced with other people occupying their Promised Land, they whined, "We are like grasshoppers in our own eyes." God had promised them victory, but they refused to do the work to claim it and own it. Why? Because they gave more credit to their imaginary self-perception of how others *might* see them than to who God told them He would help them become (Numbers 13:33).

Our enemy speaks out against us. Just like Goliath taunted, "Am I a dog that you come at me with sticks?" our enemy shouts at us, "You're just a spindly twig! You can't win! I'll snap you in half!"

Or what about King Saul? He told David, "You are not able... You are only a boy!" Have you ever heard that message at any point in your life? "You can't _____ because you're not _____. You're only _____, and that's all you ever will be?" No matter whose mouth it comes out of, that's your enemy trying to trash talk you and your God.

When the enemy tries to tell us what we can't do, let us remind him what our God **CAN** do.

Who You Truly Are

> *For God has not given us a spirit of fear and timidity, but of power,*
> *love, and self-discipline.*
> *~ 2 Timothy 1:7, NLT*

If you don't deliberately embrace your true identity and own your self-worth by receiving God's unwavering love, you will be vulnerable to believe the lie that you don't deserve victory. You must know that God intends you to be an overcomer, or you'll continue to feel like a defeated victim.

You are a warrior.

Fight fiercely for your faith. The devil will try to steal it from you or destroy it altogether. Don't let the enemy of your soul win. Run to your Warrior-Dad. He's got your back, and He will never fail you.

We conquer evil, but never in our name or by our power. We triumph over evil through putting our faith in Jesus into action. The victorious ones are those who believe in and associate with Jesus, trusting Him who already secured our victory for us.

You are an adventurer.

You weren't meant to sit on the sidelines and watch the game. There are no positions for "bench warmer" in God's kingdom. You are not intended to be a spectator to your own life.

God wants you to get out there and go after it, chase down the goal and wrestle for the prize in the mud and the rain. Anything less than a thrilling adventure leaves you restless and wanting something more that you can't quite put your finger on. God calls you to a holy adventure with Him, but you will never experience it if you refuse to get off the couch and out of your comfort zone. Victory always lies beyond the borders of the familiar places that feel comfortable to us.

You are an overcomer.

No one has promised you a life of ease and comfort. In fact, you've been warned to brace yourself for a rough ride. You are promised that though you are buffeted and tossed about, your enemy is powerless to destroy you.

If you hang on to Jesus, you might get thrown off now and then, but by His grace, He will give you strength to rise again, brush off the dust, and get back in the saddle.

Don't let the trouble overcome you. Remind yourself you were made to overcome the trouble by the power of Jesus. He has already overcome the trials and sorrows for you so that through Him you can share in His triumph.

You carry the light of Christ to a dark world.

Darkness is powerless to prevail against you. Even the tiniest light of Christ within you defeats the shadows. You need not fear the dark or whatever lurks in the shadows of your life. Jesus' light is so bright and penetrating that no darkness can stand against even a flicker of it.

> Darkness is powerless to prevail against you. Even the tiniest light of Christ within you defeats the shadows.

The blackest night is powerless against the tiniest flame. As soon as light shines, the darkness flees. So it is with spiritual darkness. The frailest flame of faith in Christ will send the dark scurrying away.

You are more than a conqueror.

We are hard pressed on every side, but not crushed; perplexed,
but not in despair; persecuted, but not abandoned;
struck down, but not destroyed.
~ 2 Corinthians 4:8-9, NIV

Whatever life throws at you, God's love is always greater, always stronger. It is impossible to be separated from His love unless you stubbornly refuse to receive it. Open your arms wide and feel His comforting and protecting embrace as He walks through the storm with you.

Trouble, hardship, persecution, hunger, nakedness, exposure, danger, sword, life-threatening diagnoses, death of a loved one, life struggles, angels, demons, our present circumstances, our fears for the future, powers that are greater than we, the height of the obstacles before us, the depth of the pits we have sunk to, or *anything else* that can possibly exist or be imagined is utterly powerless to separate us from our Champion (Romans 8:31-39).

You are victorious, not victimized.

Jesus' victory is ironclad. He is unbeatable, and He wants to share His victory with you. Don't you love it when the Olympic gold medalist pulls bronze and silver medalists up to the top tier as a gesture of good sportsmanship and camaraderie?

Jesus is forever at the top of the podium, and by comparison, we didn't even get out of bed to make it to the trials on time. But He pulls us up to the top of the podium to share in His victory that we didn't win and we don't deserve—just because He loves us and it delights Him to do so. You are unbeatable, not because you are invincible but because Jesus is.

The ultimate victory we are to rejoice in is that we have the gift of eternal life with Jesus. This is the real victory—that sinful messy people can live forever in perfection and harmony with a holy and perfect God. This is the victory Jesus has won for us!

Since our strength is in Christ and our victory is through Him, even the smallest, weakest, youngest, newest, frailest believer can stand strong against the worst the devil can deal out *if* he stands firm in Jesus and not himself.

Suit Up: Get Your Armor On

> *Put on the full armor of God, so that you can take your stand against the devil's schemes. For our struggle is not against flesh and blood.*
> *~ Ephesians 6:11-12, NIV*

God has thoroughly equipped us to be victorious spiritual warriors. He provided all we need to resist our adversary and stand strong against the evil that threatens to undo us and all we hold dear.

Gumby Soldier

During water survival training, we practiced what to do if our aircraft was shot down over a large body of water. This exercise involved a small muddy pond, a life raft, and a piece of survival gear known as a "poopy suit." Lovely name. It's as attractive as it sounds.

It's an olive-green rubber suit that covers your whole body. Only your head and hands stick out. There are very tight rubber bands at these three places to keep the water out. The idea is that you should be able to stay dry and warm for hours, or even days, in the water while you await rescue.

As it turns out, the poopy suit I was issued was not in great condition. As I swam about the muddy pond, dutifully executing the survival tasks I was assigned, water began to leak into my suit. Growing wetter and heavier by the minute, it became increasingly difficult for me to move around, much less swim.

Finally, it was my turn to be "rescued." An upperclassman hoisted me up using a small crane simulating the rescue helicopter. As my body was pulled from the water, the extent of my suit's failure became evident to all.

"We've got another Gumby!" yelled the guy who hauled me out. Apparently, I wasn't the first cadet with a disabled suit. I probably weighed at least twice my normal weight with all that water. I flopped helplessly onto the deck at the top of the crane, my limbs too ballooned out to bend.

Two guys held me upside down by my ankles while another stretched open the band around my neck. They shook me until all the water had gushed from my suit, over my face, and back into the muddy pond from whence it came. Then I was released to go on to the next "survival" activity. If the water doesn't kill you, the upperclassmen might. Just another fun day at "The Zoo"!

The very piece of gear that was supposed to ensure my survival nearly caused my drowning and also cost me a good chunk of my dignity. All the equipment in the world will not help if it is worn-out, ill-maintained, or improperly used.

Fortunately, God equips us much better than this. He has properly and completely equipped us for every good work and every fierce battle (2 Timothy 3:17).

Equipped for Victory

God doesn't just send us out into a spiritual battlefield and say, "Have a go! Let's see how you do." God thoroughly equips His soldier-saints to fight the good fight of faith without giving up, giving in, or getting captured.

Get Dressed on Purpose

Getting suited up for battle is a deliberate action. We don't get dressed accidentally. We decide what to wear around the house and when we go out. We dress differently for different occasions, depending on the need. I dress differently to play paintball than when I go to the Air Force Ball. My anticipated activity influences how I decide to dress myself, and my choices are deliberate.

Similarly, we must be deliberate about how we are spiritually "dressed" as well. We must put forth the effort to take off what is old, dirty, worn out, frayed, no longer useful or ill-fitting, and put on the new garments God has lovingly prepared for us.

> *Therefore, as God's chosen people, holy and dearly loved, clothe yourselves with compassion, kindness, humility, gentleness and patience.*
> *~ Colossians 3:12, NIV*

We have already acknowledged that we are in a war with a dangerous enemy. Knowing who we are in Christ and that we are destined for victory, we must dress as victorious warriors. Yet many of us put more thought into which pants to wear or what shoes match best than what we should wear spiritually speaking.

Putting on armor is preparation for the fight. The purpose of the armor is to give you protection and equip you with weapons, enabling you to defend the spiritual territory God has given you, and to fight and win spiritual battles.

We can have confidence in the protection our God provides. He has told us that no weapon forged against us will be able to take us down when we depend on Him for our victory (Isaiah 54:17).

> *Stand firm then, with the belt of truth buckled around your waist, with the breastplate of righteousness in place, and with your feet fitted with the readiness that comes from the gospel of peace. In addition to all this, take up the shield of faith, with which you can extinguish all the flaming arrows of the evil one. Take the helmet of salvation and the sword of the Spirit, which is the word of God.*
> *~ Ephesians 6:14-17, NIV*

Let's consider each piece of the Armor of God from Ephesians 6 in light of our understanding of the various parts of our personhood as described previously in Chapter 6.

1. **Belt of Truth** – Wrap your mind in God's truth to maintain a **Strong Mind**.

> *Every word of God proves true. He is a shield to all who come to him for protection.*
> *~ Proverbs 30:5, NLT*

Knowing, believing, and standing on the Truth is crucial to withstanding enemy attacks. The source of our Truth is God's Word. We need to be hungry for the truth. It is imperative to identify and reject the lies of the enemy. Our minds are a primary target, and if we aren't grounded in truth, we will be wounded in the battle.

We may not think of a belt as an essential item when we are getting dressed, but it was a critical piece of equipment for the Roman soldier. They had two different types of "belts."

One went around their waist, used to keep their dagger as well as to tuck up their tunic to keep from tripping over it when they ran. It also secured their breastplate.

The second belt went across one shoulder and down to the waist on the other side. In today's military attire, the "balteus" is worn primarily for ornamental practices, but a Roman soldier used it to hold his sword.

Everything hangs on a proper understanding of God's Truth. The Truth holds the rest in its rightful place and keeps everything secure. The truth also keeps us from getting tripped up. When we are intent on running our race to win it, we must learn to throw off our misunderstandings of how God works in our lives (Hebrews 12:1).

The belt also held the soldier's dagger. The Armor of God mentions the Sword of the Spirit (the Bible), which we will get to later. But the Scripture doesn't assign a spiritual role to the dagger. If you will permit me to think creatively about this application, I see a dagger as a smaller version of a sword, used for close-up encounters or when the sword is temporarily unavailable.

If the Sword of the Spirit is the Word of God, then perhaps the Truth Daggers are bits of Scripture and Scripture-based truth we have memorized and carry with us at all times. These portable truths can be used for practical everyday use and to defend ourselves during an unexpected ambush when our Bible is out of reach.

> The spiritual air we breathe is polluted with falsehoods about who God is, what He thinks of us, who we are, and the nature of the real fight we are in.

To help you get started memorizing and using Truth Daggers, I have started a list for you based on each chapter of this book. They are available online at www.StandStrongFaith.com to download, print, and share. I encourage you to add your personalized list of verses and Biblical truths that you want to carry with you at all times. God's Truth . . . Never go anywhere without it!

The biggest obstacle to knowing and applying God's truth is the constant bombardment of opposing lies we face daily. The spiritual air we breathe is polluted with falsehoods about who God is, what He thinks of us, who we are, and the nature of the real fight we are in.

The only cure for deception is the truth. We must learn to be deliberate about countering lies launched at us with God's Word. It's time to **recognize** them for what they are, **reject** them from your thoughts, and **replace** them with God's Truth. This concept is covered in much greater detail in the second book, *UNDAUNTED: Your Battle Plan for Victorious Living*, in the chapter on developing a strong mind.

2. **Breastplate of Righteousness** – Guard your heart with God's righteousness to keep a **Strong Heart**.

    Above all else, guard your heart, for everything you do flows from it.
    ~ Proverbs 4:23, NIV

In addition to our physical heart, we must be wise to protect our spiritual and emotional heart as well. It is the source, the wellspring of our life. We guard our hearts by right living in accordance with God's wisdom. Righteousness involves obedience to God and repentance when we mess up.

Bear in mind, it is impossible to earn our way into a right standing with God. The very best we have to offer are filthy rags destined for the trash heap (Isaiah 64:6). Ultimately, our righteousness must come from somewhere other than ourselves.

The tragic problem of our human condition is that even when we know the right thing to do, we do not possess the capacity, power, or sometimes even the desire to accomplish it (Romans 3:10-12). God solves this problem for us by supplying the righteousness we lack and offering us His own . . . if we are willing to accept it.

He generously credits our faith in Jesus' perfection to us as our righteousness (Genesis 15:6). It is God Himself through the power of His Holy Spirit who empowers us to live righteously. We are wholly unable to accomplish this by our own will or effort (Romans 9:16).

So the right living that guards our hearts comes from a synthesis of our desire and attempts to do what is right, and God's great mercy and grace when we fall short...again and again. When God looks upon us, His definition of "blameless" is not "perfect and without error," but redeemed by God's power and love.

Our righteousness is not based on what we've done or abstained from, but on laying claim to what He has done for each of us. We first lay claim to the righteousness that is ours by exchanging our sinfulness for Jesus' perfection and redemption (salvation/justification).

We then seek to live rightly by loving God and loving the people He has made (Matthew 22:36-40), by acting justly and loving mercy, and daily walking humbly with God (Micah 6:8, sanctification). We strive in all things to overcome evil with God's goodness (Romans 12:21).

Knowing we are incapable of getting it right every time, we must seek from God the power to discern wisely. We ask Him to show us where we fall short so that we can agree with what He reveals (confession) and turn to go the other direction (repentance).

This is how we guard our hearts on a daily basis.

3. **Ready Feet** – Stand your ground and move forward in faith with the fortitude of a **Strong Will**.

> *For it is God who works in you to will and to act in order to fulfill*
> *His good purpose.*
> *~ Philippians 2:13, NIV*

Roman soldiers had cleats on the bottom of their shoes to maintain a secure footing and reduce slippage, to hold their ground and maintain traction on rough or muddy terrain. Also, their hobnailed boots increased the durability of the sole, so it didn't wear out as fast.

Our spiritual feet must be ready to do two things.

a. <u>Stand Our Ground</u> – We are called to stand our ground and resist the devil. We are not to give up any ground to him. God will help us to stand firm, so we do not slip, falter, or fall. But when we do, because we will, we learn to get back up—rise again, brush the dirt off, and have another go by the grace of God (Proverbs 24:16).

b. <u>Move Forward in Faith</u> – Secondly, we are called to move forward, carrying the Good News of the Gospel to others who are harassed or imprisoned by enemy forces (Romans 10:15).

As the hobnails of the Roman boots prolonged the life of their well-worn shoes, we must persevere though we are weary and worn. We can't give up on doing what is right, even when it seems fruitless (Galatians 6:9-10).

Let us never slow down or stop until we cross the finish line. We can die when we're done with the work God gives us, but until then, we will keep pressing on with our eyes fixed on Jesus (Hebrews 12:2).

4. **Gospel of Peace** – Make peace with God through Jesus, and He will give you a **Strong Spirit** as you continue to abide in Him.

> *For if, while we were God's enemies, we were reconciled to him*
> *through the death of his Son, how much more, having been reconciled,*
> *shall we be saved through his life!*
> *~ Romans 5:10, NIV*

Peace is the ultimate goal of the whole war. Despite the bloody battles and the hard-fought campaigns, peace is what we all long for. Peace means the war is over and the fighting can cease.

The paramount peace our souls crave is peace with God. When we refuse to cooperate with God's redemptive plans for us, we put ourselves at war against Him. There is never a truce; if we do not submit to God's side, we are raging against Him in a desperate unwinnable battle for a misguided sense of false freedom (Romans 5:10).

However, since there is no middle ground on which to stand, the inverse is also true. When we are at peace with God, we find ourselves at war with God's enemies (the devil and his fallen angel hordes).

To succinctly summarize Chapter 6 and Chapter 8: Fight against the enemy and surrender to God, for in so doing, you will find the peace you crave.

We must stand strong on the Message of God's love for humanity and all individuals. A sure footing in the Gospel—who Jesus is and what He's done for us—brings peace and preparedness to handle whatever life, people, or devils throw at us.

Remaining grounded in Christ is our source of power. Just as the fist can't punch without a strong connection to the ground via the feet, we are ineffective and merely "beating the air" when we fail to remain connected to God in Christ (1 Corinthians 9:26).

5. **Shield of Faith** – Shield your life with an **Unshakable Faith** in God's goodness and greatness.

Since we are receiving a Kingdom that is unshakable, let us be thankful and please God by worshiping him with holy fear and awe.
~ Hebrews 12:28, NLT

Hopefully, you enjoyed Chapter 7 where we saw that God Himself is our shield (Genesis 15:1). He goes ahead of us, walks with us, and comes along behind us to protect us where we are vulnerable and unable to see the enemy. He is present in every battle we face. We never walk alone.

Faith in in itself will do nothing to protect us against the schemes of the enemy. It is what our faith rests on that makes the difference. Our faith in our unfailing God is our shield against the flaming enemy arrows (check Chapter 6 for a reminder of his tactics). He launches deceitful thoughts about God and ourselves that come at us as arrows aflame.

Our unshakable faith in our faithful God is what shields us from these merciless attacks. Use the truth of God, as revealed to us in the Scripture, to snuff out the flames of falsehood before they become a blaze that burns out of control, scorching your life with heated lies.

I have so much more to tell you about building an unshakable faith in our unbeatable God that I have to save it for a separate book! The third book in this STAND STRONG series, *UNSHAKABLE: Stand Strong Even When Your World Gets Rocked* will teach you how to fortify your faith so you can keep standing strong when life gets messy.

6. **Helmet of Salvation** – Trust your **Strong Savior,** Jesus, to protect what is most vital and to bring you safely into Eternal Life.

For Jesus is the one referred to in the Scriptures . . . There is salvation in no one else! God has given no other name under heaven by which we must be saved.
~ Acts 4:11a-12, NIV

A helmet protects our most critical organ, the brain. Life is impossible without it. Our primary preparation and protection begin with a relationship with God through Jesus. Without this, the rest of the equipment is utterly useless.

It is impossible to experience a peaceful life without first making peace with God. This is the necessary first step. Just as a helmet is essential to physical survival in battle, salvation is essential to spiritual longevity and a victorious life both now and in Eternity.

We are secured and protected in Christ by His work done on our behalf, not because of our efforts. He has clothed us with garments of salvation and the finery of His right living (Isaiah 61:10a).

Because of what Christ has done, we have hope, and we are to wear this hope in our salvation as a helmet to protect ourselves from the onslaught of a messy world (1 Thessalonians 5:8). Hope brings life. Hopelessness kills.

In survival training, the instructors told us that a person could live three weeks without food, three days without water, three minutes without air, and three seconds without hope. American POWs in Vietnam could often tell who would die next because that person had given up hope of freedom or any victory.

If you aren't sure if you've received the helmet of salvation God has for you, please pause right now and turn to the Appendix. Read *How to Join the Victorious Army Today* and prayerfully consider your response.

Suiting Up Daily

When suiting up daily to fight our battles, it is important to remember that our ultimate defense is the Lord Himself. You may have a battered faith-shield, or perhaps you've dropped your Bible-sword, and can't even find your peaceful shoes.

Don't fear! Just stick close to God. He is your shield, guard, and guide (remember Chapter 7?). He can see us safely through the battle, even when we are more Gomer Pyle than King David. *Shazam!*

Now, let's turn our attention from our defensive protection to the offensive weapons God provides for us to live victoriously.

Fight Back: The Weapons of Our Warfare

We are human, but we don't wage war as humans do. We use God's mighty weapons, not worldly weapons, to knock down the strongholds of human reasoning and to destroy false arguments. We destroy every proud obstacle that keeps people from knowing God. We capture their rebellious thoughts and teach them to obey Christ.
~ 2 Corinthians 10:3-5, NLT

In addition to a strong defense, we need offensive weapons to fight for our faith. The kind of weapons we fight with are not the same ones the rest of the world uses. If we are going to fight spiritual battles, we need spiritual weapons.

In fighting spiritual battles, our objective is to destroy fortresses of thought and belief that the enemy has erected against the wisdom, goodness, and grace of God. These "strongholds of human reasoning" and "false arguments" are the very same ones started by the rebel Lucifer long ago.

We are not so much engaged in a physical battle as much as we are a battle of competing philosophies, worldviews, and perspectives. And the contest all boils down to two essential questions:

- Who is Jesus?
- Who has rightful authority over my life?

So let's check out the weapons God has given us to use so that we may live victoriously (not violently).

God's Word Sword

For the word of God is alive and powerful. It is sharper than the sharpest two-edged sword, cutting between soul and spirit, between joint and marrow. It exposes our innermost thoughts and desires.
~ Hebrews 4:12, NLT

God's Word is not just a book. It is so much more. It is a living and active entity, infused with the very breath of God (2 Timothy 3:16). The words of God will always accomplish exactly what He intends them to do (Isaiah 55:11).

There is power in God's word. He spoke the whole of Creation into existence with only His words (Genesis 1:3-26). Jesus Himself is also called the Word of God (John 1:1-5). Jesus appears in John's Revelation with a double-edged sword coming from His mouth (Revelation 1:16, 19:15).

When Jesus found Himself weak and harassed by His enemy, He calmly told the devil, "It is written," and simply quoted God's Words. The devil had no response. After three encounters with the truth of God's Word, Satan was forced to retreat and hope for a better chance later. He never got one.

Prayer Force

Pray in the Spirit at all times and on every occasion. Stay alert and be persistent in your prayers for all believers everywhere.
~ Ephesians 6:18, NLT

Prayer is our long-range spiritual weapon. (Air Force. Prayer Force. Get it?) We can pray for the person standing next to us or a person whose name we don't even know halfway around the world. Power in Jesus' name is equally effective in both situations.

Since we are speaking with the Only One who has perfect and complete intel on all personnel and every situation, He can fill in our gaps of information and understanding. We can ask God to launch the power of His healing, salvation, and peace to any place we want while sitting in our own home.

It is through the prayers of people that God chooses to release His power to accomplish His will on this earth. This is a great mystery to us. The all-powerful and sovereign Creator of the universe has chosen to work through frail, faulty, and self-centered human beings. Nevertheless, our prayers focus His power like a laser beam to demolish the enemy's evil efforts against us.

Worship Weakens Evil

Be filled with the Holy Spirit, singing psalms and hymns and
spiritual songs among yourselves, and making music
to the Lord in your hearts.
~ Ephesians 5:18b–19, NLT

I think worship works a little like psychological warfare. It cripples the enemy's morale and his will to persist in the fight. It causes enemy "soldiers" to willingly exit the battle space without fighting. They merely give up and surrender.

There is real power in praise and worship. Our adversary becomes incapacitated in the presence of our praise. Worship of the One True Living God is Satan's kryptonite. It neutralizes his power.

The enemy can't stand in the presence of the holy God; even he must bow his knees before his all-powerful Maker. The enemy of our souls is powerless to withstand our praise of the One who always has been and always will be greater than he.

With our worship, we remind him of his original failure to maintain his rightful place of submission before the Living God. He crumples in defeat before the power of the One he can never be. The name of Jesus alone is enough to make the forces of darkness tremble and shrink back in fear (James 2:19, Luke 8:28-31).

Freedom Through Fasting

Man shall not live on bread alone, but on every word
that comes from the mouth of God.
~ Matthew 4:4, NIV

When we willingly fast from comforts and conveniences that are a part of our normal routine, it helps us shift our focus to God. We realize that we *can* go without food, or dessert, or spending money, or social media, or TV for a while, and we will not waste away after all. We learn that above all else, it is God that we crave, because nothing else can satisfy our souls and soothe our unraveled feelings the way His presence does.

We don't deny ourselves just for the sadistic fun of it or because we are "bad" and deserve it. By denying ourselves, we are reminding ourselves that our true dependence is on God alone. Anytime we have a craving or desire for the thing we said we'd temporarily forsake, it is a cue to pray and tell God how much we need Him every moment.

The time that we save by not cooking or internet surfing or driving to get our fancy coffee also creates space in our hectic lives to focus on our time with God. I find that on the days I fast, my body may be a little whiny but my mind is so much clearer and receptive to God-led ideas. Fasting and prayer often go together as each enhances the other.

Overcoming Testimony

Now have come the salvation and the power and the kingdom of our God, and the authority of his Messiah. For the accuser of our brothers and sisters, who accuses them before our God day and night, has been hurled down. They triumphed over him by the blood of the Lamb and by the word of their testimony; they did not love their lives so much as to shrink from death.
~ Revelation 12:10–11, NIV

Our testimony is our witness of God's goodness and greatness in our lives. What has Jesus done for you that no one else could have done and which you couldn't have achieved by your own effort?

Jesus healed someone who had been blind his whole life. When others questioned the man about his healing, he simply explained, "I was blind, but now I see." Religious leaders who were jealous of Jesus' popularity came after the healed man, trying to discredit Jesus.

Jesus had done an amazing thing for this man, and nobody seemed eager to rejoice with him. Instead, they accused him of lying, and his parents acquiesced to the religious leaders for fear of excommunication. Even they refused to back him up.

Undeterred, the man stuck to his guns and to the truth about what Jesus had done. Each time the opposition questioned him, his responses grew bolder and his declarations more profound. It seemed the more they antagonized him, the further he was willing to go to give glory to God.

The first time he told his story, it was just the facts about the mud and the washing. By the end, he was boldly proclaiming Jesus as the promised Messiah and daring the pompous religious leaders to contradict him. They had no reasonable response, so they verbally assaulted him again and then threw him out of the temple.

The beautiful thing about our testimony is that we don't have to have to be experts or scholars. We can just be ourselves—ordinary people with struggles common to all who are merely dependent on an extraordinary God. We can answer the mocking skeptics with, "I don't know how to answer all your questions, but I can tell you what Jesus did for me."

It is important for you to know and own your story. Think through what Jesus has done for you. What are the key turning points in your life, situation, or attitude? Practice expressing it engagingly so that when someone asks you why you still have hope after everything that has happened, you'll be ready to give God the glory. Be like the formerly blind man who grew bolder and more assured of the divinity of Jesus every time he told his story.

There is power in your story. Be ready to share it.

Your Life-or-Death Fight to the Finish

Just to recap the defensive and some of the offensive equipment we've been talking about, let's read Ephesians 6:10-18 one more time because it's just so rich. This time in The Message paraphrase.

God is strong, and he wants you strong. So take everything the Master has set out for you, well-made weapons of the best materials. And put them to use so you will be able to stand up to everything the Devil throws your way. This is no afternoon athletic contest that we'll walk away from and forget about in a couple of hours. This is for keeps, a life-or-death fight to the finish against the Devil and all his angels.

Be prepared. You're up against far more than you can handle on your own. Take all the help you can get, every weapon God has issued, so that when it's all over but the shouting you'll still be on your feet. Truth, righteousness, peace, faith, and salvation are more than words.

*Learn how to apply them. You'll need them throughout your life. God's
Word is an indispensable weapon. In the same way, prayer is essential
in this ongoing warfare. Pray hard and long. Pray for your brothers
and sisters. Keep your eyes open. Keep each other's spirits
up so that no one falls behind or drops out.*
~ Ephesians 6:10-18, The Message

And don't forget the offensive weapons of our spiritual warfare!

*We use our powerful God-tools for smashing warped philosophies,
tearing down barriers erected against the truth of God, fitting every
loose thought and emotion and impulse into the structure of life
shaped by Christ. Our tools are ready at hand for clearing the ground
of every obstruction and building lives of obedience into maturity.*
~ 2 Corinthians 10:3-5, The Message

God wants you to be strong. He's called you to stand strong, and
He's ready to equip you to be victorious. But you have to be willing
to pick it up and use what He gives you.

When Crisis Comes

*"Living by faith includes the call to something greater than
cowardly self-preservation."*
~ J.R.R. Tolkien

I have watched news reports of people who acted heroically in
response to a crisis or tragedy. I'm sure you have been drawn into
these incredible stories as well.

I have noticed a common thread. The interviewer always asks the
person what he was thinking when he risked his life to save others,
or why she stood up to the criminal with actions that said, "No. Not
today you don't." The hero always has the same answer. "I didn't have
time to think. I just acted."

When a sudden desperate situation descends on you forcing you
to react, there is no time to consider the alternative and weigh the
consequences. You just do something or . . . you don't—you freeze.

How you respond will not be determined not by what you decide at that moment (because you won't have time to decide) but by every decision you've made in your life up to that point. Those decisions of your past made you who you are when tragedy strikes. You react out of who you are as a person, not what you are thinking at the moment crisis comes calling.

So today, even when there is no crushing crisis, make the decisions that will lead you to become the person you want to be in that life-defining moment. Because when that moment comes, it will be too late to decide how you will respond or who you will be to meet the challenge.

In my moment of crisis, as I held my son's lifeless body, and in the months and even years that followed, I did not respond with faith, hope, and trust. Looking back, I don't like how I acted, what I thought, or who I became because of my personal tragedy.

I can't change the past, but I can decide what to do with today. I'm choosing to make an effort now to deliberately make decisions that will lead to a response grounded in unshakable faith in any future trails I may encounter.

I know now that God is always with me and He's always good no matter what. I know that His promises are true even when my distorted perception tries to convince me otherwise.

I'm choosing to trust God anyway, even when—*especially* when—He doesn't make sense. I'm learning to let go of the battles I was never meant to fight and to lay down the weapons of judgment and unforgiveness I've used against people. Instead, I choose to fight hard against evil forces for the preservation of my faith and out of compassion for the people with whom I share this planet.

No Victory Without a Battle

"There is no victory without a battle, no testimony without a test and no miracle without an impossible circumstance."
~Kris Vallotton

Never forget that Christ's death on the cross was an apparent defeat. It seemed the enemy of all that is good and true had won the day.

But an unimaginably greater victory was on the way. This is true for our lives too. Don't deem it all a useless failure yet. Wait for God to show up. He will always have the last word.

> *Now it is God who makes both us and you stand firm in Christ.*
> *~2 Corinthians 1:21, NIV*

God's power, not our effort or will, will keep us standing strong in Christ. It's His strength, not ours that wins the victory for us. We will not live victoriously by our might or power, but by God's Spirit alone (Zechariah 4:6).

When we are weak, He is strong, and He makes His strength known to those around us. If we are strong all the time, what need do we have of God? But He uses the weak to show the strong what real power looks like (1 Corinthians 1:27).

Learning to Live Victoriously

Maybe you picked up this book because you were feeling defeated and wanted to learn how to start winning at life. Perhaps you have found yourself in a place where faith and reality collided, leaving you with broken dreams, a busted-up heart, and a confused faith.

I hope you can see how asking seeking questions and dragging your doubt before God is okay. In fact, He wants you to bring all your brokenness and mess to Him. How else can He help you clean it up and rebuild it better than it was before?

Have you been challenged to believe anyway, even when God doesn't make sense? Did it sink in that He can be trusted to handle all things well and with great care and love?

We talked about the nature of the fight we face—who our enemy is and why we can't lose when we team up with our invincible God.

Have you identified any areas where you are fighting the wrong fight? Are you butting heads with another person, or lamenting unfortunate circumstances, or mourning the loss of a dream or a job or a relationship or a loved one?

Can you see now how your real battle is with your selfishness and pride, negative thoughts, bad attitudes, temptations to justify doing what's wrong, or a spirit of unbelief?

Refreshing and deepening our understanding of the magnitude of our unbeatable God is necessary to enable us to trust Him completely. Our surrender to His love is the gateway to our joy and peace.

Knowing who you are in Christ, and knowing that God sees you through the lens of His redemptive grace is paramount to living victoriously. You are His beloved treasure who has been created to win at life.

> *What, then, shall we say in response to these things?*
> *If God is for us, who can be against us?*
> *~ Romans 8:31, NIV*

Finally, Stand Strong

So stand your ground and keep standing in the power of Jesus. And when you fall, because you will, let Him help you back up and set you on the right path again.

You are a beloved warrior so suit up and get busy battling for righteousness clothed in compassion. Let love motivate everything you do. Get out there and meet your battle head on with the strength and power of your Champion.

You are meant for victory. Shut out all lies that try to tell you otherwise. Listen to God's voice of Truth. He loves you more than He loved His own life, and He enables you to live victoriously.

You are

- A **victor**, not a victim.

- A **treasure**, not a failure.

- An **overcomer**, not a doormat.

- A **masterpiece**, not a mistake.

God says so! Believe it and live the Truth. Stand strong and live victoriously!

> *Finally, be strong in the Lord and in his mighty power.*
> *~ Ephesians 6:10, NIV*

RESOURCES

The following pages summarize some of the material presented in this book to help you remember and apply these truths to your daily living.

These and many other resources are available as printable documents at StandStrongFaith.com.

JOIN THE VICTORIOUS KINGDOM TODAY!

In reading this book, have you realized that you are unsure if you have ever chosen the winning team? It's possible that as you read this book, you realized your life in relation to God is not what you thought it was or what you hoped it can be.

Are you ready to defect from the kingdom of darkness and join God's victorious kingdom?

Good news! As long as you are breathing and your heart's beating, it's never too late!

You will never be turned away no matter who you are, where you've come from, what you've done or haven't done, or what's been done to you.

You are always welcome, because these are the days of grace (Isaiah 55:6-7). The only "outsiders" in God's kingdom are those who choose to be. God excludes no one, but He does allow people to exclude themselves if they insist.

> *Seek the LORD while you can find him.*
> *Call on him now while he is near.*
> *~ Isaiah 55:6, NLT*

Gaining access to God by acknowledging that Jesus is who He said He was (namely God, the only perfect human, and the answer to the problem of our sin) is the starting point.

Nothing I've said in this book even makes sense until you start with who Jesus is. Maybe reading this book has increased your desire to start that journey, made you curious, or caused you to want to return to the relationship with God you enjoyed in the past.

Now is the time. This is the day. Deciding who Jesus is to you is the single most important life decision you will *ever* make. Don't put it off. No one is guaranteed tomorrow. But you are guaranteed that if you turn to Him right now, at this moment, He will embrace you, receive you, accept you, love you, forgive you, and rescue you. You've got nothing to lose but guilt, failure, and defeat but you have an eternity of perfection to gain.

It's so simple.

If you declare with your mouth, "Jesus is Lord," and believe in your heart that God raised him from the dead, you will be saved.
~ *Romans 10:9, NIV*

That's it. Just believe it and say it. "Jesus is God, and He alone can save me from the mess I've made."

> All by yourself, you are so valuable to God that there is nothing He won't do to win your heart. It doesn't take a world full of hurting people to move the heart and hand of God. It only takes one. Just you.

You've probably heard of John 3:16, "For God so loved the world that he gave his one and only Son, that whoever believes in him shall not perish but have eternal life." It's true, God loves **the whole world** but did you know that even if you were the only person in the whole world past, present, or future in need of salvation, He would have done it all (given up His heavenly glory, endured an unjust trial, been beaten, tortured, mocked, and spit on, faced a horrific death by the most excruciating form of execution ever invented) *just for you alone*?

All by yourself, you are so valuable to God that there is nothing He won't do to win your heart. It doesn't take a world full of hurting people to move the heart and hand of God. It only takes one. Just you.

We are incapable of achieving victory on our own, but that does not mean we are merely passive receptors of God's grace. He extends mercy to us on outstretched nail-scarred hands, but we must accept it to call it our own.

All who ask Jesus to save them will be saved (Romans 10:13), but sadly, not are willing to humble themselves and ask for or accept a rescue. Humans don't like to ask for help because we want to believe we are independent and in charge of our own lives. We are uncomfortable with the idea that we are not in control after all.

Imagine for a moment that you are on a boat in the middle of the ocean and notice a person struggling to keep their head above water nearby. Overcome with compassion for the desperate individual, you throw them a buoy so you can pull them to safety. Imagine your incredulous shock when the person refuses help and replies in between gulps of water, "I don't need help. I'm a good swimmer."

You look up and scan the horizon. The land is nowhere in sight. Not even a world-class swimmer could swim his way to safety from here. You know the person will drown, not because rescue was unavailable and not for lack of provision or invitation but simply because they foolishly refused the help that was offered, choosing to trust their own insufficient skill instead.

There's only one way to get to God, and it's not by your skill at navigating life.

> *Jesus answered, "I am **the** way and **the** truth and **the** life.*
> *No one comes to the Father except through me."*
> *~ John 14:6, NIV (emphasis mine)*

Some might object, "Isn't it exclusive to say Jesus is the only way to God? What if there are other ways that are equally valid? It seems hateful to tell another person that their concept of God is incorrect."

Imagine that the building you're in right now suddenly caught on fire. A voice of authority announced on the intercom for everyone to evacuate immediately and leave by any door they chose.

But what if I happened to know that all but one of the doors were locked from the outside? You could believe the door you chose led to freedom and safety as fervently as you want, but in the end, you would be trapped and consumed by the flames, because although your belief was sincere, it wasn't grounded in truth.

What is the most loving thing I could do in this situation? Would it be best for me to remain silent and let you believe what wasn't true, even at great expense to yourself? Or would the most loving action be to tell you which door provided escape and show you how to access it?

Jesus is not exclusive. He makes His unbelievably generous offer available to everyone. He has asked for volunteers because true love cannot be required, it must be freely given. He will choose as many as would volunteer. If you want to be in His kingdom, you can get in through the Door He has made available. But if you don't volunteer, you don't get picked. Not because Jesus doesn't love you or thinks you're unworthy, but because He won't force you to be in a relationship with Him if you don't want to.

When we accept what Christ has won for us, our fellowship with God is no longer hindered by the stench and scars of our sin. Jesus' righteousness has built a bridge across the gap for us, so we have free and unlimited access to The Holy Almighty God.

God's wrath against sin is real, but He has already taken it out upon Himself to spare us the torment and humiliation. He yearns for us to accept the exchange He has so graciously offered, so we can bypass the penalty we deserve for failing to hit the mark of perfect love and obedience.

If we choose to reject His substitutionary sacrifice, then we have no recourse but to pay the cost of our shortfall ourselves. This is a miserable and terrifying outcome from which He desires to rescue us.

It is by the name of Jesus Christ of Nazareth...Salvation is found in no one else, for there is no other name under heaven given to mankind by which we must be saved.
~ Acts 4:10b, 12, NIV

So what about you? Who do you say that Jesus is? Much is at stake in how you respond to that question. I urge you to consider your answer thoughtfully.

I invite further dialogue on this most urgent matter. You can reach me at elizabeth@StandStrongFaith.com.

SOUNDTRACK FOR YOUR SOUL
MY PLAYLIST FOR AN UNDEFEATED LIFE

Because Every Life Needs a Soundtrack!

Music was created for communion between God and His people. This is a list of songs that I have personally found very encouraging and inspiring on each of the topics listed. You can find a playlist containing all these songs at youtube.com/elizabethmeyers.

1. **Conflict**: *When Faith and Reality Collide*

   "Oh My Soul" by Casting Crowns

   "Before the Morning" by Josh Wilson

   "Held" by Natalie Grant

   "Praise You in This Storm" by Casting Crowns

2. **Shaken**: *When Faith Falters*

   "Strong Enough" by Stacie Orrico

   "What Do I Know of Holy?" by Addison Road

   "Small Enough" by Nichole Nordeman

   "Just Be Held" by Casting Crowns

3. **Doubting**: *When Faith Gets Confusing*

   "Never Been a Moment" by Micah Tyler

   "Blessings" by Laura Story

   "Beautiful Ending" by Barlow Girl

   "Who Am I?" by Point of Grace

4. **Believing Anyway**: *Even When God Doesn't Make Sense*
"Even If" by Mercy Me
"Someday" by Nichole Nordeman
"I Still Believe" by Jeremy Camp
"They Just Believe" by Josh Wilson

5. **The Battle**: *Know Your Enemy*
"Warrior" by Hannah Kerr
"Battle" by Chris August
"Good Fight" by Unspoken
"Whom Shall I Fear" by Chris Tomlin

6. **The Real Fight**: *Oppose Your Enemy*
"Greater" by Mercy Me
"Hard Love" by NEEDTOBREATHE
"I Will Not Be Moved" by Natalie Grant
"Higher" by Unspoken

7. **The Only Victor**: *Know Your God*
"More Than You Know" by Danny Gokey
"The Great I AM" by Philips, Craig and Dean
"Battles" by The Afters
"Hills and Valleys" by Taren Wells

8. **The Sweet Surrender**: *Know When to Give In*
"Lift My Life Up" by Unspoken
"Trust in You" by Lauren Daigle
"Sovereign Over Us" by Michael W. Smith
"Lay Me Down" by Chris Tomlin

9. **Beloved**: *Know Your Worth*
   "Remind me Who I Am" by Jason Gray
   "Wanted" by Dara McClean
   "Name" by Nichole Nordeman
   "Mended" by Matthew West
   "Unfinished" by Mandisa
   "You are Love" by Stars Go Dim
   "Broken Things" by Matthew West

10. **Undefeated**: *Claim Your Victory*
    "Same Power" by Jeremy Camp
    "Sold Out" by Hawk Nelson
    "Soul of Fire" by Third Day
    "Giants Fall" by Francesca Batistelli
    "Voice of Truth" by Casting Crowns
    "Storyteller" by Morgan Harper Nichols
    "My Story" by Big Daddy Weave

WHAT TO DO WITH DOUBT

Here are four steps we can take to overcome and diminish our doubt.

1. Accept that doubt is a fact of life.
2. Expose your doubts for what they are.
3. Share your struggles with someone you trust.
4. Surrender your uncertainty to a trustworthy God.

JESUS, MY INVINCIBLE CHAMPION

In Jesus I am rescued, redeemed, secured, protected, defended, and empowered.

I am **rescued**.

Jesus saves me because He cares for me.

I am **redeemed**.

Jesus delivers me because I can't free myself.

I am **secured**.

Jesus holds me because He loves me.

I am **protected**.

Jesus shields me because He knows my weakness.

I am **defended**.

Jesus fights for me because the battle belongs to Him.

I am **empowered**.

Jesus fights through me because my weakness displays His strength.

"I AM GOD'S BELOVED" DECLARATION

By God's mighty power and boundless grace, I am:

Beloved (Romans 8:38-39)
Redeemed (Galatians 3:13)
Beautiful (Song of Solomon 4:7)
Unashamed (Psalms 34:5)
Renewed (2 Corinthians 4:16)
Held (Deuteronomy 33:27a)
A new creation (2 Corinthians 5:17)
Forgiven (1 John 1:9)
Flawless (Song of Solomon 4:7)
Overcomer (1 John 4:4)
Uncondemned (Romans 8:1)
Free (John 8:36)
Wonderfully made (Psalms 139:14)
Strong (Daniel 10:19)
Chosen (Ephesians 1:11)
Unafraid (1 Timothy 2:7)
Part of a family (Ephesians 1:5-6)
Eternal (John 3:16)
Perfected (Hebrews 10:14)
Completed (Philippians 1:6)
Equipped (2 Tim 3:17)
Lavished in grace (Ephesians 1:7-8)
Never forgotten (Isaiah 49:16)
Unaccusable (Romans 8:33-34)
Victorious (Romans 8:31)
Held together by Jesus (Colossians 1:17)
Holy and blameless (Ephesians 1:4)
Righteous (Romans 3:22, 5:17)
God's masterpiece (Ephesians 2:10, ESV)
Priceless, worth any sacrifice (Romans 8:32, 5:8)

PUT ON THE ARMOR OF GOD

1. **Belt of Truth** – Wrap your mind in God's truth to maintain a **Strong Mind**.

> *Every word of God proves true. He is a shield to all*
> *who come to him for protection.*
>
> *~ Proverbs 30:5, NLT*

2. **Breastplate of Righteousness** – Guard your heart with God's righteousness to keep a **Strong Heart**.

> *Above all else, guard your heart, for everything you do flows from it.*
>
> *~ Proverbs 4:23, NIV*

3. **Ready Feet** – Stand your ground and move forward in faith with the fortitude of a **Strong Will**.

> *For it is God who works in you to will and to act in order*
> *to fulfill His good purpose.*
>
> *~ Philippians 2:13, NIV*

4. **Gospel of Peace** – Make peace with God through Jesus, and He will give you a **Strong Spirit** as you continue to abide in Him.

> *For if, while we were God's enemies, we were reconciled to him*
> *through the death of his Son, how much more, having been reconciled,*
> *shall we be saved through his life!*
>
> *~ Romans 5:10, NIV*

5. **Shield of Faith** – Shield your life with an **Unshakable Faith** in God's goodness and greatness.

Since we are receiving a Kingdom that is unshakable, let us be thankful and please God by worshiping him with holy fear and awe.

~ Hebrews 12:28, NLT

6. **Helmet of Salvation** – Trust your **Strong Savior**, Jesus, to protect what is most vital and to bring you safely into Eternal Life.

For Jesus is the one referred to in the Scriptures . . . There is salvation in no one else! God has given no other name under heaven by which we must be saved.

~ Acts 4:11a-12, NIV

ACKNOWLEDGEMENTS

I am grateful for the many people who have made this book possible. I only have space to thank a few.

To Jesus, who has tenderly walked with me through every shadow-filled valley and patiently led me to every mountain-top panorama. If there is anything commendable at all in my life, He deserves all the credit. Without Him, I am utterly defeated and a hopelessly broken mess.

To my husband, Joel—my best friend, partner, role model, coach, cheerleader, and confidant all rolled into one. Thank you for continuing to walk this road from trial to triumph with me. Thank you for the gift of countless hours you sacrificially served our family so I could wrestle words from my heart out onto paper. I'm so excited to be your new favorite author!

To my children—You provide the motivation and inspiration for almost everything I do. On my darkest days when my loftiest goal was mere survival, it was your sweet faces and tender snuggles that strengthened me to get out of bed, get dressed and get busy living. Thank you for your encouragement as I hammered out this book and your patience every time you heard, "Not right now. Mommy's writing." I'm excited to cheer you on as you live out the purpose for which God created you. Each one of you is such a unique and profound gift. It is the great privilege and joy of your Dad and me to share our lives with you.

To my parents—Thank you for your sacrificial love, dedicated devotion and unwavering support. You always sought to provide me with the best opportunities and pushed me to be my best and work with excellence.

To my sister, Christina—Your words were a balm to my broken heart when I hurt too much to ask for help. You inspire me to be a better person every time we talk.

To everyone else I call family and all my amazing friends—thank you for cheering me on and keeping me accountable. You are always close to my heart even when we are far apart. Thank you for believing me these past three years when I told you I was writing a book but had nothing to show for it yet.

Journeys are always better when we don't have to take them alone. Thank you for sharing this one with me.

Photo by Larissa Photography

ABOUT THE AUTHOR

Elizabeth is a veteran, the wife of a full-afterburner fighter pilot and the mother of eight energetic children. This dynamic combination leads to no small amount of chaos in her day-to-day life.

She graduated from the U.S. Air Force Academy with a BS in Human Factors Engineering and served as an officer in the Air Force until she traded in her boots for bottles and began the much more demanding and exceedingly more rewarding life-long career of motherhood.

The sudden death of her pre-born son radically altered the course of Elizabeth's life. Her resulting struggle through depression and anxiety left her undone but God was faithful even when she wasn't. Elizabeth's personal journey from trial to triumph has filled her with a passion to encourage others like herself whose faith sometimes falters in the face of harsh realities.

I'd love to connect with you!

Blog: BlessedBeyondtheMess.com

Facebook: facebook.com/thelizmeyers

Twitter: twitter.com/thelizmeyers

Instagram: instagram.com/thelizmeyers

Pinterest: pinterest.com/theLizMeyers

YouTube: youtube.com/elizabethmeyers

email: elizabeth@standstrongfaith.com

Download your free prayer resource e-book at
BlessedBeyondtheMess.com/subscribe to enrich your
daily communication with God.

THE STAND STRONG BOOK SERIES

UNDEFEATED: From Trial to Triumph
How to Stop Fighting the Wrong Battles and Start Living Victoriously

UNDAUNTED: Your Battle Plan for Victorious Living
Winning in Life by Building a Strong Spirit, Soul, and Body

UNSHAKABLE: Stand Strong Even When Your World Gets Rocked
Building a Biblical Foundation for an Unshakable Faith in an
Unbeatable God

Book Two
UNDAUNTED: Your Battle Plan for Victorious Living
Winning in Life by Building a Strong Spirit, Soul, and Body

We often find ourselves defeated because we don't understand how our spirit, soul, and body are interdependent and all require continual strengthening.

UNDAUNTED will teach you specific, practical steps to take in five key parts of your personhood (spirit, mind, will, heart, and body) to give you the confidence and courage to start building a stronger, more victorious life today and walk in the victory God intends for you.

Now you can build a winning life by having a plan to strengthen your spirit, soul, and body. Learn how to overcome anxiety and defeat depression daily so you can live victoriously even in the midst of fear, uncertainty, and painful experiences.

Book Three
UNSHAKABLE: Stand Strong Even When Your World Gets Rocked
Building a Biblical Foundation for an Unshakable Faith in an
Unbeatable God

It's easy to struggle in life because of flimsy ungrounded faith, unclaimed promises, and wishy-washy purposes. Learn how to fortify your faith so you can stand strong even when life gets messy.

UNSHAKABLE will help you learn to live with passion and purpose in spite of your pain through a better understanding of God's power, plans, promises, and presence in your life. This book will explain the Biblical perspectives on which an unshakable faith is grounded.

Knowing God's purposes in His kingdom, both visible and unseen, will enable you to weather any storm because you'll be standing on the solid Rock of Jesus' victory.

Available soon wherever books are sold!
Visit StandStrongFaith.com to get the
most up-to-date information.

STAND STRONG FAITH ONLINE

Visit the website!

Please visit StandStrongFaith.com for supplementary resources to support you as you stand strong in your faith. There you will find free printables, prayers, scriptures, playlists, and other tools to help you fortify your faith to live
UNDEFEATED, UNDAUNTED, and UNSHAKABLE.

Please email elizabeth@standstrongfaith.com
with your questions, comments, feedback or suggestions.

Share the love!

Do you want your friends and loved ones to live undefeated too? If you enjoyed this book, please consider telling others about it, sharing it on social media, or giving a copy to a friend in need.
Thank you!

Join the conversation!

Use *#standstrongfaith* & *#undefeatedbook* on social media
to share what you've learned and
how you are living undefeated!